T0311136

MARRIAGE
AS A
FINE ART

MARRIAGE
AS A
FINE ART

JULIA KRISTEVA
PHILIPPE SOLLERS

TRANSLATED BY

LORNA SCOTT FOX

Columbia University Press *New York*

Columbia University Press
Publishers Since 1893
New York   Chichester, West Sussex
cup.columbia.edu

Du mariage considéré comme un des beaux-arts
copyright © 2015 Librairie Arthème Fayard

English translation copyright © 2016 Columbia University Press
All rights reserved

Library of Congress Cataloging-in-Publication Data
Names: Kristeva, Julia, 1941– | Sollers, Philippe, 1936– author. |
Fox, Lorna Scott, translator.
Title: Marriage as a fine art / Julia Kristeva; Philippe Sollers;
translated by Lorna Scott Fox.
Other titles: Du mariage considéré comme un des beaux-arts. English
Description: New York: Columbia University Press, 2016. | [First published
in French as] "Du mariage considéré comme un des beaux-arts copyright ©
2015 Librairie Arthème Fayard"—Verso title page. | Includes
bibliographical references.
Identifiers: LCCN 2016021195 | ISBN 9780231180108 (cloth: alk. paper) |
ISBN 9780231543033 (e-book)
Subjects: LCSH: Kristeva, Julia, 1941– —Marriage. | Sollers, Philippe,
1936– —Marriage. | Marriage—Psychological aspects. | Marital quality. |
Man-woman relationships. | Love. | Sex.
Classification: LCC PQ2671.R547 D813 2016 | DDC 848/.91403—dc23
LC record available at https://lccn.loc.gov/2016021195

Columbia University Press books are printed on permanent
and durable acid-free paper.
Printed in the United States of America

Cover design: Jennifer Heuer
Cover photograph: courtesy of Julia Kristeva

CONTENTS

PREFACE

Adventure

PHILIPPE SOLLERS

I NEVER THOUGHT about getting married.

Except once.

For once and for all.

This odd and deeply impassioned adventure deserves, I believe, to be related in detail.

But what about the title: *Marriage as a Fine Art*? It harks back in ironic fashion to Thomas De Quincey's title (*On Murder Considered as One of the Fine Arts*) and to that of Michel Leiris (*On Literature Considered as a Bullfight*).[1] Most of the time, marriage is a conflict in which one of the parties winds up a victim. People get married out of calculation or delusion, time wears down this fragile normality contract, they get unmarried, they remarry, or else they stagnate in mutual disappointment.

Nothing of the sort with us: both partners equally preserve their creative personality, each stimulating the other all the time. It's the instance of a new art of love, then—something that can't easily be accepted by a broken-down society that sets great store by order. Marriage as social critique and poetic apology for freedom against every form of obscurantism? You try it.

PREFACE

Harmonizing Our Foreignnesses

JULIA KRISTEVA

A WINK AT *On Murder Considered as One of the Fine Arts* (1827–1854) by Thomas De Quincey, our title also echoes *On Literature Considered as a Bullfight* (1945–1946) by Michel Leiris. What has marriage to do with crime, corridas, or literature, you may ask? At first sight, not much at all. Are we gearing up for an ironic account of the ancient institution of wedlock, intended to secure sexuality for all, or are we going to aestheticize the shared life? Or legitimize convention?

None of these, really. We shall rather try to tell all about a given passion, with precision, without shame or shirking, without altering the past or embellishing the present, and steering very clear of the flaunting of sentimental fixations and erotic fantasies so prevalent in the current "selfie" memoir. We shall also avoid overstatement and the gothic pulp that covers for unspoken grief.

Nevertheless, when a passion spares neither distress nor aggression, it invites both trenchant density (bullfighting) and the voluptuousness of desire unto death (murder, suicide). Might marriage be the place for such an alchemy? The answer is yes, on certain conditions.

LUCK AND FREEDOMS

What were the chances that Julia (born in Sliven, Bulgaria, in 1941) and Philippe (born in Bordeaux, France, in 1936), whose respective novels delineate their incommensurable singularities, would meet in Paris in 1966? Would love each other before, during, and after May '68? Would stay married from 1967 on? The odds were so small, any calculation of the probabilities would require an astronomic amount of noughts . . .

And yet "this thing" exists. This *marriage* was well and truly registered at the town hall; and the reason it has lasted so well, with such uncompromising vitality, is because it never obeyed any law but its own. A permanent adjustment, loving and lucid, nurtured by two reciprocal and distinct freedoms.

She: more tested and secretive, with her Byzantine heritage, her foreignness as an exile of communism, with Freud holding her head above water among the eddies of globalized believing and knowing. He: craftier and more extroverted, a Girondist, a Venetian, a seducer, a libertarian, who slyly smuggles the life of the divine into the excellence of the French he impresses onto literature and politics.

We'll leave it at that: don't expect any earth-shattering revelations about the life or works of the protagonists, merely the exploration of two paths that chime and diverge and complete each other by pacing out the space, the precise and precious place, that is THEIR marriage. Accepted, constructed, dismantled, and rebuilt, incessantly, ever since this LIVING WITH appeared to them as inevitable. A place as alive as an organism: whole swathes of each of us dying, by murder or by suicide, as one or the other's freedom will have it, while others burst into life, unforeseeably, surprisingly, reticently—a never surfeited movement of starting over.

THE PLACE WHERE ONE MUST BE

You are going to approach this place through conversations. Words, reflections, questions, attitudes, and laughter are the inherent, inoperable materials of each of our identities. They are the stuff of our coexistence as a couple, then as a threesome when our son David enlarged the vulnerable space of marriage by making it one of parenthood.

To tell the truth, there is no possible meaning to any marriage other than *singular*. Neither the romantic hallucination of the *coup de foudre*—which, short of expiring in an embrace beyond time and the world, is transitory—nor the perfection of the "fusional" couple, who orchestrate everything for just one voice, will do. No, the marriage of two singularities relies less on the law that founds it than on an unshakable *conviction*, able to withstand trials as well as the joys that are not in short supply elsewhere or additionally. The conviction that "here is the place where one must be."[1]

The "name" of marriage has become—across our two lifetimes—the reality that recreates us, "perpetually suspended like a grace and an invisible menace, like the substance that nourishes and bathes each thing but does not mingle with it." It does not staunch the pain of renunciations, of sacrifices, of death blows, of passing rebirths inside or outside it; it does not negate our animal reflexes, our mindless bestiality and instincts, our decays, sicknesses, and cares, or our certain death. In marriage and with it, these upheavals pass the relay to a supreme tie, the only possible one because it is clear-sighted, which holds me *in the place where I must be*.

A MAN, A WOMAN: TALKING

In what language? Those languages it has been given us to learn and tame and modulate. So as to make more than a shield of our attuned discordance, rather a source-place that maintains, *separately together*, two beings who are not the dupes of war and peace between the sexes. But who try to *think them through, with their whole bodies*—isn't that something? In order to live, give life, and render bearable the fact that it will end. Refusing to let "both sexes perish on their own" (as feared and prophesied by Auguste Villiers de l'Isle-Adam and Marcel Proust).

The pages that follow resonate with current anxieties around the topic of marriage, while not falling for the unlikely merger of two into one or hinting at a happy solution to the idyllic, and failed, "togetherness" of "diversity." They invite you, simply but ambitiously, to ponder the experience of marriage as one of the fine arts.

MARRIAGE
AS A
FINE ART

1

COMPLICITY, LAUGHTER, HURT

LE NOUVEL OBSERVATEUR: First of all, what's your definition of love?

PHILIPPE SOLLERS: That word is used in such a ragbag of ways, to suit all the varieties of modern sentimental commerce, that one might flinch from it with embarrassment or contempt, like Céline, for instance: "Love is infinity made available to poodles." But still, it's a serious question that merits an answer. One word I dislike is the word *couple:* I've never been able to stomach it. It implies a whole literature that I loathe. We're married, Julia and I—that's a fact—but we each have our own personality, our own name, activities, and freedom. Love is the full recognition of the other in their otherness. If this other is very close to you, as in this case, it seems to me that what's at stake is harmony within difference. The difference between men and women is irreducible; there's no possibility of fusion. The deal therefore is to love a contradiction, and that's what is so nice. I'm reminded of Hölderlin's lines: "The dissonances of the world resemble lovers' quarrels. Reconciliation lies in the midst of strife, for whatever is parted is reunited. The arteries of the heart split apart and reunite, all is life, one, eternal, and ablaze."

JULIA KRISTEVA: Love has two inseparable components: the need for closeness and constancy and the dramatic imperative of desire that can lead to infidelity. The love relationship is this subtle blend of fidelity and infidelity. In literature the figures of the love relationship vary widely: from the romance of courtly love to the crude, intense probing of the modern period. Everything that defines our civilization, in terms of its meditations on sex and feeling, is based on the faithful/ unfaithful axis.

NO: But how can you associate fidelity and infidelity?

JK: First of all, let's try to define fidelity. One could call it stability, protection, long-term reassurance. Is fidelity a dated topic, a hangover from the past or our parents, a quaint relic fit to be swept away by the pressures of modernity and the power of desire? I don't think so. I'm speaking as a psychoanalyst here: the infant needs two figures, two *imagos* without which it can't face up to the world. The mother, of course, but also the father, who is less often mentioned: the father of the earliest infant identifications. Not the forbidding, oedipal father, but the caring father. In our later experiences of love, we are also searching for variants of those two images. There lie the psychic requirements for fidelity. Once in possession of these bearings, these elements of stability, it's possible to free up one's sensory or sexual relationships and give desire its head.

PS: I get impatient with the systematic reduction of infidelity to the sexual aspect. In the space of one century we've moved from regarding sex as the devil incarnate to having it foisted on us, technically and commercially, as something indispensable. Sex is supposed to be the truth, to be all there is to say about people, while ignoring the rest: the persistence of feeling through time, the relationship's success in the mind.

Our society, which used to treat sex as fiendish, is now making it compulsory and deadly dull. I've often been accused of writing novels that whip up this sexual inflation themselves. But that's exactly wrong. I've always shown sexuality as lightly as possible, in a detached, ironic way, like a self-aware fancy that one can take or leave. I mean, sexual infidelity doesn't cut much ice with me. There are worse things.

JK: I think sexuality has been understood as essentially a revolt against conventional norms, and this was no doubt necessary in a society where religious or puritanical prohibitions were oppressive for individuals. These days, though, you hear a lot about retrenchment into the private, reverting to the rules. It's certainly a step backward, into a form of conservatism. But it also marks a greater awareness of what the sexual revolt was finally about. It had a meaning, which was liberty. But also a nonmeaning: the destruction, oftentimes, of the self and the other. In male-female relations, you can engage in "outside" friendships that are sexual and sensual while still respecting the body and sensitivities of your main partner. That's what being faithful means. It doesn't mean never being apart or never knowing another man or another woman.

PS: Can we add to that the word *trust?* I was very impressed by this wonderful phrase from Vivant Denon: "Love me, which is to say, don't suspect me."

JK: The danger in "love me but don't suspect me" is that it's really saying "be my Mom" or "be my Dad"; the idealized "mother" and "father." Many couples who claim to be faithful, and indeed are an absolute storybook picture of devotion, have become frozen in maternalism or paternalism. For those of our generation who handle their joint life differently, it looks like a frightful game. At the same time, one wouldn't deny that infidelity packs some horrors of its own. It is always an ordeal. It can wound; it can deal lethal blows. But you can also laugh at it.

PS: I want to say that faithfulness is a kind of shared childhood, a form of innocence. Here, in a nutshell: we're children. If we stop being children, we're unfaithful. The rest—the encounters, the fits of passion—doesn't matter very much, in my view. True infidelity resides in the congealing of the couple, in heaviness, in the earnestness that turns into resentment. It's an intellectual betrayal above all. While we're on the subject, I must stress that I don't believe in transparency. I'm against the kind of contract agreed between Sartre and Beauvoir. I'm all for secrecy.

JK: The sentiment of fidelity goes back to childhood and its longing for safety. Personally, I consider myself someone who had reassurance lavished on her as a child, and that gave me a lot of confidence. When I was younger, I did feel bad when faced with sexual infidelity, but I can't say I experienced it as a betrayal. In fact, I don't feel that I can be betrayed. Or, to put it another way, treachery doesn't really get to me. Even though, unlike you, Philippe, I don't believe secrets can be preserved. Everything comes out sooner or later.

PS: I was talking about the honesty ideology in certain couples.

JK: Let's be clear: female humans don't have the same sexual and emotional interests as males. Men and women feel a different jouissance, just as their attitudes to power, society, and offspring are different. We two are a couple formed of two foreigners. Our different nationalities accentuate something else, which people often try to avoid seeing: men and women are mutual foreigners. Now, a couple who takes on board the freedom of these doubly foreign partners can turn into a battleground. Hence the need for harmonization. Faithfulness is like the harmonization of foreignness. If you allow the other to be as foreign as you are, harmony returns. The squawking becomes part and parcel of the symphony.

NO: Were the affairs you both went in for an explicit precondition of your union, or was it circumstance that led you one day to break the pledge that most young lovers make to each other: to be faithful forever?

JK: We never made that pledge.

PS: And we weren't all that young when we met. Julia was twenty-five, I was thirty. May '68 happened almost straightaway. It was a period of intense experimentation, in minds, in bodies. There were no contracts in those days. Freedom spilled out of its own accord.

JK: At the end of the sixties, which were the years of our youth, there was such a freedom in love relationships that what people call infidelity was not regarded as such. Today we live in another era, a time when unemployment, the dwindling of political activism, and the fear of AIDS all contribute to the new focus on coupledom and fidelity.

PS: History ebbs and flows. There are periods of opening and periods of closure. The restless liberty of the eighteenth century, then the Terror, then the Restoration. Intense mobility between 1920 and 1940, replaced all of a sudden by *Travail, Famille, Patrie*. A huge positive mutation around 1968, followed by fifteen years of numbness, drift, and now, finally, regression: witness all this anxiety and gloom.

JK: Yes, we're certainly in a period when security considerations trump everything else and there's little economic autonomy. One can't indulge in a libertarian attitude to infidelity without a minimum sense of inner security. Plus, needless to say, of financial independence—which women, despite their efforts, are still far from possessing.

PS: Julia and I are completely on a par economically. In the absence of that prerequisite, there's not much use in talking about the sophistications of love or the ins and outs of fidelity.

JK: We're discussing the behavior of financially independent individuals. Otherwise we couldn't have this conversation at all.

NO: You mentioned the famous contract between Sartre and Beauvoir, which stipulated that they would tell each other all about their extramarital adventures . . .

PS: I think that with them this honesty pact was actually a form of reciprocal inhibition, like signing a contract of joint frigidity. My own conviction is this: When you're really into someone, you keep it to yourself. Besides, we don't know how Sartre really ran his life, in what compartmented, watertight way . . . My feeling is that he, out of generosity and also indifference, let people say a lot of things. He had his clandestine life. It's rather a pity he didn't write about it. I can see him managing it on the sly. In any case, there's not a female character in all his work who's truly interesting. Nor in Camus either, nor indeed in Malraux. Nor in Aragon. What a century! I've learned a great deal more about women from Proust [*laughter*]. In reality, the whole business is pretty unconvincing.

JK: Sartre and Beauvoir were libertarian terrorists. Their books still display an intellectual and moral daring that is far from being understood or surpassed, even now. To carry out their work of libertarian terrorism, they turned themselves into a shock commando unit. This commando relied on their shared history as two wounded people. On the one hand, Sartre's oedipal wound, what with his absent father and then his anguish at being so brilliant and yet so ugly. On the other hand, there's Beauvoir, with her virile ambitions, her cold intelligence, and, I daresay, her depressive sexual inhibitions. And despite all that, they did something wonderful: they showed the whole world, to its dazzlement and envy, that a man and a woman can live together, talk together, and write together. You have a go, see if it's easy! But their terrorism consisted in setting fire to anyone who ventured anywhere near their precious twosome and turning them into victims. Their famous "transparency" was like a charter of the powerful against the rabble of aspirants. Still, their relationship, which is unrepeatable, is to be interrogated; it shouldn't be demonized, surely.

NO: What about Aragon's relationship with Elsa?

JK: The myth of their couple protected him, in the same way as their membership in the Communist Party. There can be many reasons for joining a party, but in Aragon's case it was clearly a way of ensuring himself against sexual risks. Against the distress inflicted by his own infidelity, in fact. He had a heartbreaking affair with Nancy Cunard that drove him to the verge of suicide and that he papered over in his worship of Elsa. Here is an ambivalent, unhappy instance of the sham couple, with extra poetry on the side. Other forms emerged following the death of Elsa Triolet, when Aragon owned up to his homosexuality. But we mustn't forget the magnificent passages he wrote before that, on the female body and female jouissance, in *Irene's Cunt*. Where he somehow cannibalizes the feminine, gobbling it up from inside. In this kind of infidelity tale one must keep in mind the bisexuality of both partners, which makes standard fidelity even more difficult. There again, truths that aren't easily acknowledged.

PS: Bisexuality, there's a subject with a future [*laughter*]!

JK: It certainly is! Although most people try to hide their bisexuality behind a mask, everybody's thinking about it.

PS: I used to visit Aragon at home sometimes. Elsa Triolet was always barging unexpectedly into the study where we were chatting. It was strange. One day, she signed one of her books for me: "To Ph. S., maternally." We never saw each other again.

NO: Another couple who made a mark on their time was Danielle and François Mitterrand.

JK: The mythical representation of coupledom responds to a social need. The unity of the group, especially a national group, is nurtured by the fantasy of the primordial union, the parental pair. This original cohesion myth, cracks and all, is what the political apparatus throws at the "popular masses" like wool over their eyes. We saw that in vaudeville mode in the United States, when rumors of Clinton's cheating tainted—and rebooted—his career, and in Britain with the Charles and Diana saga. Nowhere but in France will the wife be seen standing next to the mistress at the funeral of a president.

PS: It would have been way more revolutionary to see at least three women—or five or ten, why not?—lined up for the funeral scene. Two comes across as rather stingy, a bit petit bourgeois, I find. France can boast of a grand tradition in that line. It deserved better. I felt let down, frankly. Mitterrand once told me he was a reader of Casanova. He seemed to be on the right path . . . Well, if the Americans were shocked, that's something, at least!

NO: At the beginning of the century, the philosopher Jacques Maritain and his wife Raïssa swore an oath of abstinence. Wasn't that a lovely way of keeping desire intact?

PS: Desire, what desire? You're forgetting the third partner in the matter, namely God!

JK: Belief in God seems to steady a great many couples. The question is, who takes God's place, now that people don't believe anymore. I see quite a few people on the couch who replace God with the cult of arts and letters. Many couples who work together replace him with their business . . .

PS: Saying to each other: Let's abstain for the good of the business [*laughter*]!

NO: So would you prefer, to Maritain's faithful abstinence, the all-consuming passion extolled by Denis de Rougemont in *Love in the Western World*?

PS: There's no whys or wherefores to passion. Fidelity responds to the question why, but passion is unjustifiable. Passion does what it wants, for good or ill. Rougemont's thesis, as I recall, remains out-and-out romantic—Wagnerian. Amorous passion as inescapably leading to sacrifice and death. It's a highly structured ideology and still hugely powerful today. As if passion necessarily had to be punished, as if love could only end in disaster. I object to that notion, quite violently. That's not my idea of love. I'm more "*Mozart for ever*,"[1] as Godard put it; I've never been a Wagner man. No gloom, please. Fidelity, infidelity, those are concrete, social questions. Nothing wrong with them. But passion is redolent of a different era.

JK: Passion aspires to the absolute, while at the same time calling the absolute into question. We're helpless against the violence of its excesses. They belong as much to the order of pleasure as to the order of destruction. Passion is enthusiasm and the proximity of death. It is joy and it is death. It is annihilation and jubilation. It is Shakespearean. An explosion, a fragmentation outside time. Whereas fidelity is inside time. I think Rougemont goes back to the pre-Freudian, premodern experience of love. From before Picasso, before Artaud, or, if you will, before sex shops and drag queens. It's impossible not to know, these days, how fundamentally perverse and polymorphic sexuality is.

NO: Have you ever thought that one or other of you could succumb to passion, and are you prepared to fend off the unjustifiable, should it happen?

PS: In case you hadn't noticed, let me point out that we're in the middle of a *grande passion* right now [*laughter*]!

JK: We're so imbued with ourselves, as individuals and as a couple, we find it hard to imagine that kind of situation [*laughter*]. Or at least to imagine any passion that could jeopardize the understanding between us. Things can be difficult when one parallel affection emerges more strongly than others, but due to our tacit philosophical collusion the other relationship fades out, or maybe it persists but in a lower key. My female patients often say, "He betrayed me" (men don't complain so much; they're too proud). As an analyst I understand them, but not as a person. To feel betrayed implies zero self-confidence, a narcissism so battered that the slightest affirmation of the other person's individuality is felt as a crippling blow. The least mosquito bite has the impact of a nuclear bomb.

PS: To me, the idea that one passion contradicts another is a deplorable piece of sloppy thinking. I always see it as a throwback to the religiosity that poisons this kind of thing. The word *passion* should be employed in the plural. Up with the plural!

JK: Well, yes, but that assumes an individual who isn't "one," a plural individual. Is everyone able to live out several passions at once? I'm not sure they are. You're speaking from the viewpoint of an artist or writer. The standard individual aims for a coherent, unified ego. The passions he or she experiences tend to cancel each other out.

PS: Well, I call that a mistake. Endless romanticism, endless nineteenth century . . . None of that stuff holds water today, I don't think.

JK: Some people repress one passion to choose the other: they have an unconscious. Others separate and accumulate: they're the polymorphic ones. I feel closer to the first. I guess I'm more conservative than you.

NO: But have you ever felt jealous?

JK: I don't like other women enough to be jealous of them. It may be my problem, but still, what a relief!

PS: I say likewise: I'm not sufficiently attracted to men.

NO: While unfaithful men raise a smile, adulterous women are still severely judged. Has the lifestyle revolution of the last thirty years changed anything?

JK: Only on the surface. Feminism, along with the development of libertarian ideologies and the advance of technologies such as contraception, helped to liberate female sexuality. But I'd say that women are still being held back. A woman who gives free rein to her sexuality is tolerated, so long as she doesn't have any other assets. But, if she exercises so-called responsibilities or has a good brain or is in a position to make a difference in social matters, as soon as she indulges her desire she becomes perceived as a threat. She becomes worse than unfaithful—she becomes a slut. That word is off limits these days, people use terms like *unconventional* or *erratic* or confine themselves to a knowing smirk . . . Most of the women who have been brought down in French political or media circles owe their disgrace to gossip or slander about their sex lives. There's still this assumption that a woman must have slept her way to the top.

PS: Why, the staying power of that prejudice is appalling, it's a secularized form of religious mania. Even so, I think that women's scope for choosing their partners has considerably increased. And the more financially independent they become, the freer they'll feel to assert what they do and don't like.

NO: Choose their partners, yes. But have they really been accorded the right enjoyed by men, to have several partners at once?

PS: A certain degree of concealment remains the order of the day.

JK: Women obstinately prefer secrecy, no doubt to protect themselves. They won't be caught shouting their affairs from the rooftops, the way men do so readily. This fear of female sexuality, this disapproval arises from the need for security. Society clings to the maternal image of a woman as someone who stays home to look after us. That's why as soon as a high-profile woman indulges in sexual freedom, we feel threatened. The need to be kept safe by a faithful woman is deep-seated in *Homo sapiens*, in the archaism of the human makeup. We're beginning to cast off this image, but there's still a long way to go!

NO: To confess one has strayed or to keep it a secret, that's the great dilemma for the couple even now.

JK: I don't believe there can be secrecy, at least not total. Our skill at decoding sensations and behaviors is extremely subtle, and one can easily grasp a situation without it being spelled out. Besides, there's no shortage of sneaks and gossips to spread the news. So, one always knows, definitely. Now: to tell or not to tell? Or, if you prefer, to confess or not? One can say things in a wounding manner, and one can say them in a way that shows respect for the other person. We've all met the kind of hyperliberated couple who detail each fling to the other with such sadomasochistic relish that the relationship finally breaks down. "Making a clean breast of it" can conceal the desire to crush both the secondary and the primary partner. It's best to examine one's personal motives first. Why tell? To what end? It's often impossible to keep an affair secret, but honesty where that's concerned is just as much of an illusion. A certain analytical attitude to passion is required, therefore.

PS: I'm all for secrecy (it so happens that one of my books is called *The Secret*) or at least for the utmost discretion. I don't believe humans should ever have to justify their sexuality. It's entirely their own responsibility. There's no need to mention it, unless it is making them sick, in which case they're welcome to go lie on your couch. One may be accountable in social, material, intellectual, emotional life—but never in sexual life. The notion of sexual control is inadmissible. I think, too, that social surveillance always tends to want to curb individual sexual freedoms. Totalitarianism was a nightmare in that respect, but the radiant democracy we are promised is given to repressive lurches all the time. At the present historical moment, one senses the resolve to bring us back to heel by whatever means, including religious fanaticism, closing in from everywhere. Secrecy is therefore necessary. It's the very stuff of liberty. Now, let me amuse you with a dash of Kierkegaard, from his *Diary of a Seducer*: "As a woman, she hates me; as a talented woman, she fears me; as one with a good mind, she loves me." Isn't that splendid?

JK: Kierkegaard hijacks everything, doesn't he [*laughter*]! Coming back to secrecy: it can protect, for sure, but it can just as well harm not only the person who is shut out but also, in another way, the "secret" pair themselves, huddled away in their asocial mystique. Lucidity is relevant here. I feel that people who have encountered analysis, and that includes those who've only read about it, are better at harmonizing the murderous side of their desires and the violent part of their passions. One mustn't idealize freedom. Freedom can be lethal, too.

PS: That's exactly why it's so frightening and why people sometimes kill in its name!

NO: Does your closeness have any value as a model for others?

PS: A model? No. It's just a personal adventure.

JK: A model of discordant harmonies! Nothing to do with the idyllic image of the perfect couple who never exchange a cross word, that's for sure.

2

INNER EXPERIENCE
AGAINST THE CURRENT

PHILIPPE SOLLERS: I like the title, "Inner Experience Against the Current." In "inner experience" the word to watch is of course *experience*, because I expect, or hope, that everybody here enjoys an inner *life*, despite the massive violence with which the general current opposes any such thing these days. This inner experience, then, means the experience with the person in here, which has been going on for a while, though also for a very short time, in view of the intensity of that experience. We shall have to say what kind of fundamental experience we are talking about: experience of what? To do with what thing, what object? Etc. Nothing spiritual, nothing mystical, none of that global charlatanry around the lucrative commodifications of the word *inner*. Experience being a form of knowledge, we shall attempt to say what knowledge is implicated here.

Next: "against the current." The current of what? Of the society of the spectacle, that's what, another name for this ongoing globalization, universal interconnection in so-called real time, deaths in real time—but what do we mean by "real time"? Data designed to lather the brain of anybody who would wish to learn something under his own steam.

This devastation will chiefly affect, not just human interiority, but also what is most precious to the human being: his language. For years and years now, from the beginning, the emphasis we've placed on this experience of language has seemed to us the most important thing. It's increasingly rare to come across anyone who truly *reads* anything, who hasn't succumbed to the flatness and impoverishment of instant communications.

So, to establish a context and give Julia a chance to respond, to say what she has to say upon the subject, I shall simply table the question of childhood. "The childhood we revisit at will," as Baudelaire said. Because childhood is, I believe, the location under greatest pressure today, the most highly monitored, the most damaged in its very fibers. Because childhood is decisive for the genuine constitution of inner experience. It so happens that, for swimming "against the current," you can't do much better than the two unrepentant children sitting in this very room, for reasons that are historical first and foremost. Julia is a child who went through the experience of totalitarianism. She lived in Bulgaria, under the former Soviet regime, and she underwent a traumatic experience, the death of her father, which she related in a very fine book called *The Old Man and the Wolves*.[1] I met her as a person just emerging, escaping, from a totalitarian experience. I found that tremendously intriguing and impressive, and it made me ask her over and over again about her childhood.

For my part, something is always denied me, because there weren't that many childhood experiences like mine in France: I had the great privilege of being born, shortly before the Second World War, into a thoroughly Anglophile Bordeaux family. When the German Occupation began, the Germans were always downstairs, having occupied all of our houses, and then they flattened a property in the Île de Ré because it got in the way of their coastal batteries. I heard German spoken a great deal during that period; while in the cellars, or the attics, we were listening to Radio Londres, "The French talking to the French." For a child, it was utterly decisive to belong to a family whose guiding principles—very oddly and unusually for Vichy France—led them to bet on London. "The English are always right"—that's what they said at home. So, Radio Londres, the admirable broadcasts of the Free French in 1940, with their coded messages. "Here are some personal messages . . . " I was six years old, listening to those nonsensical phrases that really struck the ear of someone destined to be a writer: "I like women dressed in blue. I repeat: I like women dressed in blue." "We will roll across the lawn. I repeat: We will roll across the lawn." All against a crackling background of interference, you know? Like that.

Two very singular childhoods, then. And so here we have, sitting next to each other, two stubbornly unruly and unrepentant children who chucked their papers, their countries, overboard. Julia is familiar with the slogan I recite to her from time to time: Vichy-Moscow, neither Vichy nor Moscow. Much as I say it, much as I repeat it, it's like I'm never really being heard.

COLETTE FELLOUS: Do you sometimes feel that you've loved each other through the telling and the experience of your two childhoods?

PS: The love encounter between two people is the rapport between their childhoods. Without that, it doesn't amount to much.

JULIA KRISTEVA: You're right to begin with childhood, because ours were so different, and yet we've brought them into tune.

Is it because I was born in a totalitarian country, is it because I was a little girl—rather than a little boy—adored by her father? All through my infant years, my one longing was to grow out of childhood, and I took my desires for realities while being convinced that my father only had eyes for me. Accordingly, his literature and gym and swimming lessons, our outings to soccer matches and to the theater, even our heated arguments made me believe that I belonged in the world of adults . . . Shoulder to shoulder with her husband, who had studied theology before doing medicine, Mom had had to give up biology and its Darwinism to devote herself to her two girls, but never tired of repeating to my sister and me that she didn't want to sit on us like eggs, but to "give us wings." In Bulgarian, *ne zakrileni* ("hatchlings") rhymes with *okrileni* ("having wings"). It's her who taught me that the fastest way to travel was not in an airplane or a rocket but in thought; she went over my math with me so I'd win the school competition . . . And, in spite of all this, I can't remember wanting anything but to grow up and make Dad proud of me; to escape from childhood and embark on that "winged" (*okrilena*) life my mother lacked. Which everybody around me lacked, in a country where "nobody lacked for anything"— communist equality guaranteeing the minimum required to get by for the population at large; but people felt infantilized by the daily worries and by the single line of thought. Anyone who spoke up got sent to jail and even to the camps. One had to grow up in order to escape . . .

The first stirrings of puberty, in sentimental intimations and idealistic daydreams, led to solitary pleasures and greedy kisses rather than sexual discoveries. It was like childhood regained, a time of abandon and innocence, protected by its covert complicities; and it was in these teenage romances, which ended up pitifully damaging for most of my girlfriends, that I accepted myself as a child. Playful, mischievous, outside time, fulfilled. A kind of childhood secreted by those fleeting, clandestine moments, boundless yet transitory. Is there such a thing as the one original childhood? Isn't it, instead, always to be experienced anew?

In any case—coming back to your political remarks—when we met, Philippe and I, two years before May '68, it was not so much France and the French language I discovered—because kindergarten with the Dominican nuns, then the Alliance Française, and then doing Romance philology at Sofia University for my doctorate had more than acquainted me with both. The surprise was that sexual explosion and my long-awaited liberation. The affinity between us was obvious from the start. And that word, *obvious,* sends me back to the childhood theme, in the sense I was trying to explain: a childhood recovered in retrospect, via an encounter, that makes one brand-new again, renascent as a different person according to the obviousness of the magnet-lover (*aimant-amant*); that makes one relive a sensory memory retrieved, revealed, and suddenly more intense, renewed. This is the base. Given this base, an existential complicity that is intellectual, cultural, professional, and lasting through time becomes possible. For me, the foreigner, this chiming with Philippe's infant self made me feel I could relate to what he embodies, what sustains him: the French language and mindset, the history of France . . . Of course, I'll always be this semi-integrated foreigner. However, in the love that rekindles our confided childhoods, and nowhere else, I cease to be a foreigner.

My entrance into psychoanalysis can only be understood as the prolongation of that infantile obviousness we were lucky enough to recreate together. After all, wasn't it on found-created childhood that Freud based free association and the transference/countertransference link? The analysand is invited to excavate their childhood—and the events of their whole life—and thus to mature step by step, baby to child to teen to parent, etc., on the analyst's couch.

I want to say a few words more about the stamp left by totalitarian communism on these infantile traces.

When I set out to talk about women's liberation, I chose the provocative term of *female genius*—taking Arendt, Klein, and Colette as examples. It was meant as an invitation to each of us, female or male, to cultivate their creativity in order to resist—"against the current"—today's ongoing massification: now that we all belong to some "community" (women, gays, bourgeois, proletarians), out goes the individual, as though we'd forgotten that liberty is a singular noun. The figure of Hannah Arendt came self-evidently to mind; I couldn't start with anyone better than the author of *The Origins of Totalitarianism* (in three parts, "Antisemitism," "Imperialism," and "Totalitarianism"). My father had just died, three months before the fall of the Berlin Wall. Instead of the simple operation he needed—while the operating suites were out of surgical thread, apparently—my father was killed in the hospital: they used to conduct experiments on elderly people. We couldn't bring this Bulgarian citizen to France while his post-operative condition was deteriorating. After that, I was told that he'd have to be cremated rather than buried, as there was no more room in the Sofia cemetery and anyway the graves were reserved for communists, in order to prevent crowds of believers from gathering; my father was a devout Orthodox Christian. When I offered to pay for a grave in hard currency (dollars or francs), the answer was that it would be feasible, since I was fairly well-known, but only if I died first . . . in which case my father and I could be buried together.

PS: With your husband!

JK: Anyhow, the world has turned this dismal page, now only relevant in the lamentable case of Cuba and especially China— although some sectors of the left are still pretty intoxicated by it, especially in France, clinging to past "gains" and digging their heels in against reform . . . But other phenomena are on the rise, tending toward the *automization* of the human species. Hyperconnection, virtual reality, the digitization of human memory, genetics, bio- and nanotechnologies, robotics, etc.: no previous generation has ever been exposed to such swift and far-reaching upheavals. New technologies are able to alter reproduction, repair organs, and increase life expectancy. Everything is changing: family structures, gender relations, and the very notion of sexual identity; our attitude to writing, books, language . . . These facilities and velocities have a downside. "Talking points," e-mail, SMS, blogging and tweeting create the mirage of a new bliss, that of the hyperconnected loner in a so-called virtual community. The Web has no outside or inside, and is open to every kind of use—consumerism, pornography, propaganda, "social" networks, collective outrage over this or that, sundry radicalizations, not to mention decapitations, to lure you in, to manipulate you ... Are you on board? You may think you are, but you're nowhere, there's no "you" anymore, just the floating, the surfing, the falling to bits . . .

That said, I don't share the despondency of those who predict the end of a world that has surrendered so willingly to technology, to the Internet, to fanaticism. On the contrary, I make Colette's conviction mine: "To be reborn has never been beyond my strength." This wager on the possibility of starting over has deep roots in the European continent to which I feel bound, after my voyage from Sofia to Paris, and even more since I began traveling the world from New York to Beijing, from Buenos Aires to Bergen, and found myself always homing (back) . . . to Paris!

Rebirth: there's no better way to swim against the current of mass leveling and automation of bodies and minds. The possibility of being reborn exists in Judaism, and in a different way in the Greek tradition. It was transfigured by Christianity; the humanism of the Renaissance and then the Enlightenment opened it up to everyone; finally, Freud had the insight to adapt it to the traumas and pain of the analysand. It parallels the certainty that troubles and sorrows are what make us think.

My life in Bulgaria had not blinded me to these rebounds, but nor had it convinced me that I myself might be capable of this trajectory of survival. And it was Philippe's vitality, coupled with his evident wounds, that locked the erotic and intellectual understanding between us into the irrefutable alchemy for which we only possess one word, *love*—even though the experience of it is plainly unique to each person and moment, with no common yardstick between them.

Ever since our first encounters, I was struck by his modernity: it resides in that lively wit and footballer's body and in that taunting laugh, the frequent scourge of the society of the spectacle, which can only take it for dubious whimsy or gratuitous frivolity or who knows what reactionary pathology. I soon realized that the light-hearted repertoire, the "joker pose," were his whole personality and exceptional, unclassifiable, immoderate oeuvre. However, I really got carried away by his "countercurrent" because I also perceived—not that

he makes any bones about his sources—how well it accorded
with the dynamic of Ulysses the seaman, with the humor of
rabbis reweaving the joy of the Torah, and with the depth of
the transfiguration wrought by Christ.

Having arrived in Paris with five dollars in my pocket, bursting with brave but hazy ideas, I had the good fortune to meet
someone who stayed by my side and who stood out in that
rather dreary French panorama, with its petty and grand bourgeois, shivering at the loss of Algeria, reluctant to face up to a
changing world, and harangued by de Gaulle amid as much
booing as cheering. What a country! I had to stay. With him.

One incident will give you the picture. We were in front
of La Coupole under pelting rain, I was staring at the water
pouring down, I must have looked preoccupied: visa problems,
grant problems, I don't recall. All of a sudden you said: "Not
worth bothering about tiny puddles. Jump!" I realized I wasn't
alone and that I could do it: I could jump. Or more accurately, I
could *travel myself*, in the neologism that a heroine of my novels
would invent. To put it in other terms again, my tendency is to
spade away at the death drive until hollowing it right out, but
you gave me the courage to lean on your dramatic vivacity—you
know that I know how dramatic it is—in order to jump over the
puddles as well as the more daunting obstacles.

PS: One thing: going "against the current" doesn't mean going
along with something that's very trendy at the moment and
wide open to hijacking as well, indeed is hijacked all the time,
namely all that prosopopeia about decline, how it's all going
to the dogs, etc. Why is our critique nothing to do with that?
Because it's full of positive counterproposals. The critics who
warn about creeping vacuousness, apocalypse, and so on are
actually part and parcel of the system, the media lap up that

kind of thing, just to compound this sort of regression that's pretty much accepted by everybody. I'm not going to go into the political state of affairs, there's no point, everybody knows about it, and this is just the beginning, wait and see where we're headed! What's absolutely fundamental to everything we do is the counterproposal. All of our books present one, whether in a novel like *Women* or essays like "Female Genius." There lies the crux of the matter, and hence a certain ambiguity appears, a sort of veil, because you're talking about the media: yes, I do think, unlike every species of puritan, that one has to know how to use the media, and I enjoy nothing more than to meet someone with major listening vibes, for example, Colette Fellous when she shows up with her Nagra, and then we make little programs that last forty minutes and go into the archives. That's it: archives, counterarchives . . . We do TV! We do counter-TV. We do radio! We also do counter-radio. We are doing an event in public here today, and at the same time it's a counterevent, because we're saying things we don't usually say or that have different repercussions.

CF: One gets the feeling, too, that you're springboards for each other. I'm thinking of that memory you have of the day you said to Julia, in front of a puddle, "Jump!"

PS: About the "Jump!" there are memories in common. What she remembers is that it was raining, she was depressed, and I told her "Jump!" What I remember is loads of other things, but it's true that that was one of the first things I said to you as we were walking down toward La Coupole, was it, or not far off, we were headed for the Rosebud, rue Delambre—how many evenings . . . Right, enough of that. I told you something else too, I remember it well. Very firmly, I said: "We shall lift the ancient curse!" Remember?

JK: Not only do I remember, but I've just received it on my Black-Berry, in the form of a rather peculiar question. Tomorrow, at Paris-7 University, there's an all-day event organized by my friend Bernadette Bricout, vice president in charge of cultural activities, entitled: "Julia Kristeva in consultation on the topic 'Speak to Me of Love'." We've just changed the title to "Is There Such a Thing as Modern Love?" But it comes to the same. So, here's the question sent in by somebody who's going to attend the improvised "consultation": "How did you manage to lift the ancient curse of the sexes?" The strangest coincidence, don't you think? I don't know if we managed to lift it, that old curse, but we certainly tried our best.

CF: I like your puddles story, because I had something similar with Philippe, one day when I was feeling low, in your office, I think, and I said: "I'm fed up," and you replied: "Now, let's see . . ." And then you said: "Do you know how to swim?" I said, "Yes." You said: "Well then, you're OK!" So there's always this idea of water, currents, the urge to struggle, to fight back, to be free, within a flow that must constantly be analyzed and reviewed. I was just wondering, in fact: Do you have conversational rituals, like do you discuss the news together at the end of the day?

PS: Colette, we're pursuing a conversation right here in public that's gone on for forty years. It never stops. We can't say, it's this in the morning, afternoons it's that, while in the evening . . . It's a conversation. I very much like what they used to say in the nineteenth century, or before: "Adultery, according to the English, is a criminal conversation." Well, I conduct criminal conversations with my wife [*laughter*].

JK: Ah! When the wife *is* the mistress . . . In any case, we're not going to tell you everything today, so let's remain on the philosophical level, swimming against the current.

CF: There's also *Inner Experience* by Georges Bataille: a text that can't be avoided and that no doubt also forms part of your bond, your coming together during those early *Tel Quel* years. How would each of you describe your own inner experience today?

PS: I'm seventeen or eighteen, I'm in Bordeaux. I'm visiting this old bookshop where there are books all over the floor. I bend down and my eye lights on a book called *Inner Experience*. The title intrigues me. It's by a writer I've never heard of—Georges Bataille. It came out during World War II, a time when in the midst of historical insanity there's a weird character writing a book called *Inner Experience*, a rather dated book, in fact, that prompts considerable upset. He is going through a real experience and he refuses to use the word *mystical:* that's what's so interesting. Let me mention in passing that Georges Bataille, someone I told Julia about immediately—she didn't know him, I don't think, though she had heard of Blanchot and others—Bataille, then, published two books in 1955 which I found completely mind-blowing, especially one of them, I can see myself reading it now, about the caves of Lascaux, discovered in 1944; the other one was on Manet, a painter you can check out this very day at the Musée d'Orsay, having a sort of resurrection, given that the last Manet exhibition was in 1983. Georges Bataille, *Inner Experience*, Lascaux, Manet: vistas opened out . . . And, of course, along with Bataille came the figure he always talked up with something close to idolatry—as I'm rather prone to do myself—namely, Nietzsche. And that went against the current of those days, because Nietzsche was commonly regarded as a fascist. Nietzsche was Nazis, and Bataille came over as a bit murky or disturbing: his erotic writings, *Madame*

Edwarda, dreadful stuff. Thoroughly unedifying: not just Nietzsche, but Sade into the bargain. So then we started to publish *Tel Quel*, and Bataille would drop in at the offices of this quarterly that was sowing such alarm among the editorial and ideological milieus of the day. What was he after? Why did he come and sit in that office? He'd take a chair, he never said much, except for one thing I remember very clearly, he said: "Ah . . . at the lycée, they used to call me 'the brute.'" What a magnificent poet! His blue eyes, etc. You won't dispute that by the time you and I met—it was in 1966—I'd already published a book called *Event*,[2] which Barthes wrote about; we'll return to that later if you don't mind. I encouraged you to read a number of things, more in depth, let's say, than you previously might have done. You were twenty-five. Utterly brilliant, like nobody else at that age, astounding, even. Yup, astounding: Let's marry her [*laughter*]!

JK: Deeply impressed is what I was . . .

PS: It must be said that, before the puddle and the jump, well, Julia shows up with her communist passport, and, as she falls ill right away with a deadly serious hepatitis, before getting her into a hospital room—it was the Hôpital Cochin, I recall—I was with you in A & E, the wait went on forever. Meanwhile the fascist press, *Minute* and so forth, were painting her as a KGB agent infiltrating the country, you know, Elsa Triolet–style. No way, not like that at all: Elsa Triolet and Aragon, what a tired old movie! When we got married, actually, it was funny, we had two witnesses and we all went to La Bûcherie for lunch, and miraculously—we'll move on to Lautréamont anon: "In the new science, each thing comes in its turn, so excellent is it"—who should be sat next to us but Louis Aragon and Elsa Triolet, holding a rather closed-circuit conversation.

We were lumbered for years with Communist Party propaganda to the effect that I was the new Aragon and Julia Kristeva the new Elsa Triolet. Wrong: no more than Simone de Beauvoir and Jean-Paul Sartre. As wrong as the ravings of the far right. Wrong: there's her, there's me, and it has nothing to do with the others, though of course we take those others into account.

CF: And you, Julia, what about your "inner experience"?

JK: At the time I didn't ask myself any questions, I was "traveling myself" . . . But now, I do wonder how I did it, arriving out of the blue like that, an unknown from a little-known, backward country, how did I ever cope with all the turmoil . . .

PS: Your French was fantastic; you were—you still are—absolutely amazing.

JK: Sure, my French was good . . . But, before I embark you all on those crossings with me, just to hear Philippe reminisce about that period—the Parisian milieu with its intrigues, its communists, fascists, publishers, writers, journalists—brings home to me, once again, and more clearly than ever, perhaps, in the presence of all of you here, how sheltered I was. In spite of culture shock, hard times, malicious gossip, rejections, and false gratifications. And what sheltered me? You, of course, your presence. You played the game, carried the can, taught me the ropes, explained the maneuvers. But I remained an outsider, I didn't get involved, I didn't belong to that "world." My professional life—from college to psychoanalysis, via writing, essays to start with, then novels, published by *Tel Quel*, Seuil, and finally Fayard—unfolded in a space apart, away from the cozy bubble of Saint-Germain-des-Prés. More and more, in fact, due to my frequent commitments away from Paris: teaching in New York, Washington, Boston, and elsewhere. In short,

I had—and still have—the advantage of being kept abreast of Paris ways, the city's blessings and impasses, everything that foreigners naively associate me with. In reality, though, I was—I am—free of it: precisely because we maintained *two* distinct social spaces, two psychic spaces, autonomous and discrete, never merged but always with something to tell each other . . . A couple? Yes, but . . . two in one, duplicated unity, yin and yang, perhaps. This precious independence also means solitude, an aloneness essential to the "mystery" that was billed as the title of tonight's event; necessary to *inner experience.* So . . . [*silence*]

JK: As you well said, a long tradition precedes us, a mostly Catholic memory, of which Georges Bataille reminds us by turning it upside down. On pain of overburdening our talk—forgive me if that's the case—I can't avoid, now that we're here in this ancient Cordelier monastery, and to clarify my intellectual procedure which is inseparable from the "shared life" people are so curious about—I can't avoid dwelling yet again on certain key moments of European culture. This culture made us the way we are, even if the disillusioned Europeans we've become are not as proud of it as we ought to be. And in this culture *experience* is THE fundamental notion. It is with and around experience that was forged the *free and infinitely constructible/deconstructible subjectivity* that has been corrupted or abolished, separately and in parallel, by so many crimes and fratricide wars including the Inquisition, colonialism, and the Shoah. Yet it remains the great value to be defended during this time of "loss of values." Apologies for the long exposition. To return specifically to experience itself . . .

I already mentioned the *heteronomy* of my family. On the one side, the theological training of my Orthodox father, strongly imbued with Greek mythology, Platonism and Neoplatonism, French and German philosophy—Voltaire, Diderot, Rousseau, and of course Hegel; and the Russian novel. On the other side was my mother's Darwinism, grafted onto the memory, long extinct among her ancestors, of the mystic Shabbetai Tzvi . . . Bulgaria is more than the home of rejuvenating dairy products, the Rose Valley and the essence of roses that perfumes grieving hearts and the universe. It's the only country in the world that celebrates culture with an Alphabet Day. May 24 is the feast day of Cyril and Methodius, the brothers who created the Cyrillic alphabet. Schoolchildren, teachers, librarians, writers, and artists parade through every town and village with a big cut-out letter of the Slavic alphabet pinned to their smock, shirt, dress, or jacket. Each person becomes a letter, and so did I, and that was the first *experience* that I perceived as such: being a letter among a host of letters . . . Before attempting to elucidate how European culture posits and develops that notion, from Plotinus to Freud, among others, may I pause a moment on that particular experience, on the echoes it awakens?

PS: It's very important.

JK: I was a me outside myself, merged with a letter that was inserted into a word or a sentence made of other bodies, other "me's," other letters. Disseminated through a festive community with its songs, its scents of roses and peonies . . . There were no people anymore, and yet this took on meaning; the grammar inscribed a message; I was taking part in this writing that transcended me, that regulated an extra world, while also being engraved on my body . . . "A rule that cures everything" (as Colette, whom I would discover later, wrote), and can even cure one of communism . . .

This experience mingles with other memories or maybe dreams, I'm not sure. I'm by the Black Sea, it's coming nearer, about to sweep me away; I grab my father's hand, and he saves me from drowning. I've never forgotten that first sensation of the loss of self. It's the moment that precedes and conditions the emergence of the new "you," the new "other" . . . Then the dream changes: I'm clutching a letter of the alphabet, clinging to its curlicues and propellers; the letter reassures me, I feel proud of myself . . . When I wake up, I reflect that this dream uses two moments experienced in real life in order to repair some tiny slights, humiliations, or rejections that hurt me and that I had to get over. Like when I wasn't allowed to carry the school flag on Alphabet Day, because my parents weren't communists, or when I was turned down by the Russian and the English high schools for the same reason; or when I couldn't study for a physics and astronomy degree in any of the "closed scientific cities" of the USSR, because they were reserved for the Russian nomenklatura. I never shed tears over those failures, I held on to my safety buoy: alphabet, books, curiosity . . . Were they a consolation? More of a direction to take. It was the same in Paris, in the ups and downs of personal relationships, professional disappointments, skirmishes at *Tel Quel*, upsets at the university or in psycho-Freudian circles . . . That dream kept on recurring.

With this foundational experience, and not yet familiar with Bataille's *Inner Experience*, which you got me to read in our first months together, I filled my intellectual knapsack by foraging through the history of philosophy, then borrowing from Freud . . . That alluvium of dreams and letters, barely noticeable during my semiological period, resurfaced at tough times. Like many women, before the Simone Veil Act of 1975, I went through the ordeal of a clandestine abortion, which put me in the hospital. All I had in my small suitcase was a toothbrush and two volumes of Hegel: *The Phenomenology of Mind* and *Science of Logic*. I was lulled by the twists and turns of the *negative*, transported to something like joy by the power of Hegel's ideas on the polyphony of experience. It was only later, when impatience, anger, and indifference were beginning to take it out on love itself, and I'd already become a psychoanalyst, who knew from Freud that the best way to rescue love is to lie it on the couch while continuing to write about it, that I immersed myself once more in mythology, Platonism, and Neoplatonism, in order to go back to Hegel and Heidegger and gain a better understanding of the transference/countertransference Freud passed down to us. A book resulted, *Tales of Love*,[3] that deals with nothing but *experience*: in the Song of Songs, Plato, Baudelaire, Stendhal, Bataille . . . and Spielberg's *E.T.* . . .

ps: Here we go . . .

jk: Back in Sofia I'd read *Hegel's Concept of Experience*,[4] the Heidegger text that had just appeared in French. A friend brought it me from Paris. As you know, it constitutes an introduction to the *Phenomenology of Mind* (1807), which laid the groundwork for the "science of the experience of consciousness" that ultimately developed into *phenomenology*. Heidegger comments and expands the Hegelian concept of consciousness as *a movement that apprehends itself, that detaches from itself*, and insists on the *emergence of a new object* in the course of this trajectory: he stresses the "tending-toward," the "path along which we are escorted to . . ." A capital moment of experience: the "new object" is not *this one*, *this* friend, say, who is there before me in this room; as I look at him, a "new friend" appears to my consciousness: this emergence *is* experience. Experience means that I lose the certainties my senses and consciousness entertained about this friend prior to seeing him here tonight. Over there I see Chairman Vincent Berger and my friend Bernadette Bricout; a brief glance takes them in as a pair of neutral bodies, abstract photos. On the other hand, if my gaze is that of an experience, then I see them, for example, as being among the friends who accompanied various intense moments of my life—Bulgarian friends, *Tel Quel* friends, New York friends; at that point I register them in the complex memory of my emotional experience. I question them, agree with them, or dispute them. As a Freudo-Lacanian, I may also, in this renewed apprehension of my friends, include loving passion and also an unconscious "hatelove" (nobody's immune from that one, though Bernadette and Vincent score better than some).[5] They appear in my consciousness transformed, at the exact moment of this exact encounter when I lose certain facets of them and of myself, so that a new apprehension of their alterity and my identity may take place. Hegel, endorsed by Heidegger, puts it admirably: there is in experience an "absolute Good Friday." To be clear, "God is dead" means everything except that there is no God. The reasoning is subtle: God, even when dead, doesn't disappear, and he can begin again. The same goes for consciousness as for experience: it vanishes only to begin again, loss and renewal; so long as it is an *experience*, consciousness *lives*; the life of consciousness involves the construction-deconstruction of unity-identity, whether it be that of consciousness, the subject, or the object. Perpetual rebirth.

cf: We're not so far from Freud . . .

JK: Quite right, Freud is not far off. The Freudian unconscious, particularly attentive to Hegelian negativity, adds a new stratum to interiority: the emergence of the *new object*, for the experience of the subject that I am, must come into play via the logics of unconscious "primary processes," urges and affects . . . New stakes, at the intersection of life sciences and sciences of the mind, arise at that point for the person who is the theater of an experience . . . But they arise also for the compartmentalized disciplines inside our compartmentalized knowledge systems, whereas *experience* urges us to be interdisciplinary.

Thus understood, experience presents a new challenge for humanism, so long as humanism refuses to consider itself a moral system fixed by the Renaissance, the Enlightenment, and the positivism of the late nineteenth century; so long as it attempts to integrate this interdisciplinarity, without forgetting the onslaught of reinvigorated, fanaticized religions. The *multiverse* of the "life of the mind," the complex dynamics of *psycho-somatic experience*, promise riches liable to revolutionize the conception of the human, in abeyance today. Linking up with the traditions that precede us, but also proposing an alternative to that aggressive, efficient and yet constricted mentality encouraged in us by hyperconnection.

To rethink *inner experience* from this angle is not simply an epistemological challenge. I've brought it up because I want to say that, with all the revolutions going on, it's the love experience that matters. We could do with a lover's discourse able to take the measure of the intimate by locating it in that interaction we call experience, able to constitute it as creativity, starting over, and renewal.

I hear you object: Has inner experience resorbed *narcissism?* What happened to *identity* and its quest for the ideal?

Have they lost their way in the meanders of an identity attracted by the magnet of the unconscious and the other, definitively hateloving and innovative?

At the heart of love, Freud places *narcissism* ("I" regards himself as the one and only object of care, safeguard, and affection; failing that, he allows himself to be captivated by the narcissism of his partner) and also *idealization* ("I" finds in the beloved an "ideal of myself" that "I" cannot live up to in and for himself; at best, it is the encounter, the bond, that constructs an ideal state, project, oeuvre). Neither the hesitations (autoeroticism versus narcissism) nor the leaps and bounds ("primal identification with the father of prehistory," "ideal of the self," "need to believe") can be understood without returning to the genealogy of the Narcissus myth.

CF: This myth has become an omnipresent reality.

JK: It's not enough to condemn the "supersize ego" of this or that political or media celeb and the me-me-me of popular fiction. Omnipresent as it is, the so-called narcissistic experience has nonetheless changed its shape through history.

It came on the scene courtesy of Ovid, in the first century of our era. Narcissus is the contemporary of the God-Man, of the religion of the incarnation. The desire to know oneself, instilled by Roman stoicism, reverted into a painful fable: the human Narcissus can only love his own image, but it is an inconstant one, vanishing into water. Lacking a stable identity, prey to one lure after another, unable to know who he is, Narcissus kills himself. Linking the gaze, the image, the inability to love others, and suicide, the text transmitted by Ovid anticipates the difficulty in forming bonds and the "autistic" inadequacy that threaten, as they did the humid torpor of Roman Europe in decline, our current virtual, screen-fixated society. What is to be done?

Plotinus, a contemporary of Narcissus, offered a Neoplatonist solution. The inmost space or "heart of hearts" of Western man was created when he, dissatisfied with the tête-à-tête of self and image, replaced this disastrous narcissistic showdown with . . . the joined hands of prayer. It's futile to contemplate your reflection in elusive representations, is roughly what he said; instead, seek your identity in and through the intellect (νοῦς or "*nous*"), carve it out "face to face with yourself": become another by the light of the intelligible. Only by dint of questioning and arguing, dialoguing with yourself, will the space of subjective interiority be opened out—for good (self-knowledge) and for ill (the complacent pathos of TV soap operas, say).

Since then, over the course of four hundred years, the biblical grafted onto the late Roman eventually produced Christian theology and its apogee in the *inner experience* of St. Augustine. His greatest transports, in Milan or Ostia, were only possible because he introduced into Plotinus's prayerful contemplation the loving ardor of the Song of Songs in which we hear, for the first time ever, a woman, the Shulamite, speak to her king (or shepherd) about God. From then on the interiority of the man of faith grew frenzied and extravagant, verging on psychosis, and many saints gladly wallowed in those extremes; but the same interiority attempted, often successfully, to clarify, channel, and rein in the new madness of love by making an ideal of perpetual self-surpassing, faith, and reason—but failing to guard against murderously dogmatic deviations.

So what about sexuality, in this vast program?

PS: Aha . . . [*laughter*]. Here we go again!

JK: You didn't think I'd forgotten about sex? Underlying, denied, condemned. Sublimated into music and painting and literature.

Restrained within marriage, exploding into transgression, libertinage, and crime. Freud straightaway saw it in the "polymorphous perverse" infant, and associated Eros with Thanatos, the death drive, not to be confused with erotic aggression. Bataille's work pushes the boundaries still farther in this respect, restoring its full potency to the destructiveness inherent in the amorous bond, in the sadomasochism of the primal scene, which the majority of mystics wove into their aura . . . If God himself arouses, according to Freud, "the deep emotion that comes from childhood," it's because experience is struck by the *unknown* and "overturns everything in us like a violent wind." Very few of those who made suffering sacred ever renounced it. Teresa of Avila was one, thanks to the joy her raptures gave her. Another was Meister Eckhart, by conceptualizing this alchemy in a lexicon he would bequeath readymade to German philosophy.

I'm nearly done, Philippe; I know, I've been talking too much! I just want to add that sadomasochistic sexuality always lurks in the background of the love experience, including that of couples. Aside from the option of denial, in the manner of puritan morality, there's no other way of appeasing it than to elucidate it without end. I don't see exhibitionist autofiction cutting through this madness inherent in the logic of desires; instead it flatters and perpetuates it. But you, you went in for the Enlightenment style: you avoid misery in your books (as Lautréamont advised), suggest the impossible in short, succinct tales, steer clear of the "universal reportage" Mallarmé hated so much, and think in a poetry alive to concepts. It's not just a literary prescription, it's the way you live: tightly, caustically, mixing irony and fun in daylight clarity and keeping all the rest under wraps. As for me, I'm curious to know and to elucidate, in order to get in touch, to touch. My novels serve to filter through what I call "metaphysical detective stories" my rebounds and survivals, reconfigured and transfigured; deliriums in "vibrating mode," never "at a rush" (as Céline described his own procedure); tireless reevaluations of belief and knowledge.

CF: After hearing your account, Julia, we can see very well how this "inner experience" came to fill an inner space you've been building since you were a little girl. That Alphabet Day was a collective event, but not everyone who took part became a theoretician of language or a writer or a poet. The outlook of an already creative child can permeate the rest of its life. I expect it was the same for you, Philippe—that the world you perceived as a boy was already sustained and magnified in you by imagination, creation, art . . .

PS: Two things strike me in the current conditions of general anthropological rumination, human, human—*human, all too human*, as someone said. First, the staying power of what everybody seems constantly to be reading, the family saga, to my mind the most ghastly brew, unless spiked with wholesome Freudian venom; we are drowning in family sagas, there are six hundred of them a year, all "me-me" as you say, but of the most constricted kind when it's in the shape of family drama. Historically speaking, there's a dozen reasons for it, I won't bother listing them. I'll just mention that there would be a lot to say about Europe and European guilt, and this, as I've explained, owing to the Anglophilia of my family— I want to be sure to get that point across—I didn't share. I feel completely and utterly innocent of the extermination of European Jews and the totalitarian catastrophe across the continent. Meaning that there could well be—in however inaudible a form—a counterproposal to be made, a totally revolutionary one to boot, that Denis Diderot, who talks to me now and then on the phone, knows all about. To return to what I wanted to say after listening to you, we are seeing the family saga make itself comfortably at home again, as if it had never been analyzed. And then, no less staggering, in the same context, is the extraordinary overrating of sexual hang-ups. Sexual hang-ups proliferate, as everyone thinks they have access to the alleged wonders of sex. In just a few years, this matter has grown extremely interesting. There's a dreadful inadequacy everywhere, and if you have the knack of depicting it, like Michel Houellebecq, for instance, does, you will immediately find a captive audience. This is the first time that it's been acknowledged and laid out flat, so it's hardly surprising if there's a tsunami of general conformism.

Coming back to the singularity of experience, which can only reach, of course, an individual in a family, the case of that individual will be exceptional, he will keep quiet and learn to be cunning, because he will feel like an exile in this world; he'll be a metaphysical being, a foreigner. After that, two singular foreigners meet, have loads of things to talk about from their own singularity and carry on talking in the form of a marriage that's unlike any other.

You brought up Hegel, rightly I think, and now, if you agree, I'd like to leave Europe, leave the West. I have an image of us during the magnificent summer, summer of 1967, you must remember. You were reading Hegel and so was I . . .

JK: And *Science and Civilisation in China*, by Joseph Needham . . . On the Île de Ré, on the beach of the Conches, under the lighthouse of the Whales . . .

PS: In a famous formulation that can be applied every day to everyone one meets, Hegel said: "To see what little contents the mind is to measure the immensity of its loss." If you're content with what happens, I have nothing to add. Anyway, while reading Hegel, the *Phenomenology of Mind*, the *Logic*, and some Lautréamont on top, you were writing your *Revolution in Poetic Language*. It was wonderful weather, we ate grilled fish and spent hours on the beach, and we also read *Science and Civilisation in China* by Joseph Needham, whom you met. China's pull for us is not a recent thing. Why did it beckon two singularities, in France, in 1966–67? And in depth, mind you: to do with China's poetry and painting and calligraphy and thought. But not just China, there was also the attraction of Sanskrit, which you worked on, as did I. How come that at such a time, after the disaster of the already declining twentieth century, two singular minds, who seldom encountered minds they could communicate with, were already interested in China and in what today are called "emerging countries"? Please, tell us about Needham.

JK: I shall talk about him with all the more feeling and pleasure for seeing a special face among our audience, Marian Hobson, who's been a dear friend of mine ever since our student days . . . and a fellow of the British Academy, where we recently coincided; she's the person who introduced me to Joseph Needham. Along with Émile Benveniste, who opened my eyes to Indo-European linguistics, Needham and his monumental work were decisive for me, for us, in providing in-depth support for our Chinese yearnings—it's important to spell this out, because nowadays people are saying all kinds of things about our Maoism.

CF: Excellent idea!

JK: I'd read an article by Needham in an academic journal, then Philippe Sollers and I had bought the first volumes of the veritable, indispensable encyclopedia he directed, and I was bowled over by the specificity, originality, and unfamiliarity of logic that underpin Chinese scientific thought. In a different way than the admirable Marcel Granet in *La Pensée chinoise*, Joseph Needham explores Daoist and Confucian beliefs and inventories the specific contributions of Chinese models to the study of matter, optics, the body, astronomy, mathematics, geometry, and more. A biologist at Cambridge, a Christian and a socialist, he became interested in Chinese science, learned the language, surrounded himself with a glittering constellation of Chinese scientists and thinkers, directed the Sino-British Science Co-Operation Office in Chongqing, traveled the length and breadth of the country, and amassed an extraordinary trove of documents that would form the basis of successive volumes of *Science and Civilisation in China*. After the war he returned to Cambridge—where Marian was an undergraduate, then a research fellow and professor, and often invited me—and around the time I met him (1967, I believe) he was appointed Master of Gonville and Caius College. I was startled and delighted by the elegance, humor, and generosity of his welcome.

We met again in Paris; he was attentive to the cultural, scientific, and civilizational mainstays of our curiosity about China, a curiosity that drew us into the political commotion and upheavals besetting Chinese Communism at the time. I never discussed the "Cultural Revolution" with him; the expression made him smile, I thought, with a mixture of benevolence and skepticism. In the aftermath of May '68, Needham showed solidarity with the students, though his decision to sponsor a fete—rather than assign the same sum to college grants—was sharply criticized by a student organ, the *One Shilling Paper*. I recall that incident as symbolically revealing of a warm, convivial man who balanced rigor and anarchism and whose free-spirited gaiety always prevailed over convention. He could tell I wasn't about to become a sinologist or start campaigning for the Cultural Revolution. But he encouraged my desire to immerse myself as much as possible in Chinese "science and civilization" as a way of broadening my research into language as experience. I signed up for a degree in Chinese at Paris-7, while taking private lessons with François Cheung. "Splendid! Writers and intellectuals will come around to it sooner or later," Needham said cheerfully.

CF: A visionary?

JK: The trend was already apparent: even in Bulgaria, before I left, one of the foremost critics, Tzvetan Stoyanov, a dear friend of mine, had written an imaginary dialogue between Lao Tzu and Confucius. The discrepancies between the two Chinese masters could be read as an emblematic expression of the political and ethical issues that lay behind the crisis of communism. As for Joseph Needham, I found out much later, in a posthumous biography of him, that he'd been manipulated by Soviet agents during the Korean War and fooled by trumped-up evidence of the American use of biological weapons in the conflict; he was blacklisted by the CIA as a result, *persona non grata*. Still, in the end his skepticism would prevail and detach him from the ideological dragooning to which so many Western intellectuals of his generation had fallen prey. Be that as it may, I remain indebted to a work that continues to enlighten me whenever I seek to grasp, with the modest approximations of a nonspecialist, the particulars of Chinese thought, history, and society.

CF: On your return from China in 1974, you wrote *About Chinese Women*.[6] Did Chinese women seem to you a source of hope against totalitarian bureaucracy?

JK: The way both men and women are steeped in the Dao, their adaptability to social, financial, and political fluctuations—presently relayed by wholesale hyperconnection—are just as likely to tip Chinese society into chaos as to bring about an automation dispensing with all concern for truth and freedom. That assessment is not the same as disillusion, nor am I predicting the apocalypse. I'm pointing to the latent and the potential, trying out hypotheses against which I'm quite sure that countercurrents and antidotes exist, including the *inner experience* that has gathered us here tonight. Might China, its intellectuals and students who are presently turning toward Europe and our human sciences, our art and literature, and even to psychoanalysis, be able to join up—in their own way—with the necessity, imposed on us, of *transvaluing* the Greek-Jewish-Christian-humanist heritage with its Muslim graft? In order to refound the principles of freedom, dignity, and autonomous subjectivity and reevaluate the social bond? The creation of the Institute for Advanced Studies in European Culture, at Jiao Tong University, directed by Mr. Gao Xuanyang, of which I am honorary president, allows us to hope so . . .

PS: I almost never hear intellectuals talking about Europe. They're not in Spain, they're not in Italy, they're not in Germany, they're not in Holland, and to conclude, they're not anywhere. Europe has vanished. Europe has gone under, guilty as it is of an appalling crime . . . One has to feel guilty to accept such a denial! I, therefore, put my foot right in it, on purpose: I don't feel guilty! Globalization on the rampage challenges Europe's writers and thinkers: Get a move on, what have you got to say for yourselves?

CF: I'd like to go back to what you were saying, Philippe Sollers, and you, Julia Kristeva, with regard to Freud. At what point did Freud appear on your path?

PS: A final word about the denial of European culture. It is a glaring consequence of America's dictatorship in every domain. The colonized Europeans are the foremost lackeys of that worldwide dominion, a vise we have to try to loosen by any means we can.

JK: My father had a book by Freud in his library, the only one, I believe, to have been translated into Bulgarian before the Second World War. I hardly dared approach the incandescent spot, as Freud was reputed to be the epitome of decadent culture, sex, and the bourgeoisie; he was mentioned very rarely, and in veiled terms. It was you who got me to read him in French, before, during, and after Lacan's seminars. Philippe was our shrink, an inveterate reader and champion of Freud. I can still visualize the pages you underlined and annotated . . .

I came back from China with two desires, to write a book about Chinese women—as you reminded us, Colette—and to become a psychoanalyst. The evidence was clear: the political strategies that claimed to jettison the dogma of Soviet totalitarianism and instead draw on national cultural specificity were part of the potential of that Chinese thought I was trying to fathom, but it lay dormant under the lid of a dogmatic regime. The promises of Western democracy left us free to test our loving and thinking beneath the wing of certain institutions (universities, publishing houses . . .), and yet those establishments also circumscribed, in an underhand way, the daring moves, the risks I felt like taking in my life. Being an exile had given me the taste for them, almost a sort of mandate. Teaching, research, and writing itself benefited from those freedoms, but they still displayed the hallmarks of their institutions. It seemed to me that psychoanalysis was the only discipline that would be able to decipher "the China" inside me and reveal my unknowns to me before I set off for the unknown elsewhere.

So I went to see Lacan. He had been due to form part of our *Tel Quel* "delegation," along with Philippe Sollers, Roland Barthes, Marcelin Pleynet, and François Wahl, but had pulled out at the last minute. "We know each other too well for me to consider an analysis with you," I said to him. "Could you recommend one of your colleagues?" Straightaway he produced the name of his last mistress's lover. Had he forgotten that I'd happened to witness a stormy scene between the three of them, shortly before our departure for China, where she'd been supposed to accompany us? Was he trying to tell me that anyone starting analysis in his school would be expected to engage with its incestuous networks? This was not the way I saw things, so I applied to the Paris Psychoanalytic Society on the advice of a linguist friend, an excellent connoisseur of Freud and of psychoanalysis, Ivan Fonagy—you knew him as well, Philippe. His son, Peter Fonagy, a member of the IPA,[7] has lately emerged as a recognized authority of British psychoanalysis in London. Ivan Fonagy, the father, is . . .

PS: . . . Hungarian . . .

JK: Yes, and very close to the Hungarian school of psychoanalysis, from Šandor Ferenczi to Imre Hermann. I don't know whether he'd had analysis himself, but his thinking was certainly steeped in it. A communist, he realized that the confessions made by the defendants in the Hungarian Stalinist trials, after the war, had been extracted under duress.

PS: Same as in Moscow . . .

JK: Absolutely. Except that Fonagy uncovered the truth because he was an experienced linguist. Hungarian is not an Indo-European tongue, I know nothing about it and can't begin to explain how a linguist managed to spot the lie. But he noticed at once that the "confessions" were expressed in the third person, not the first: it was therefore a pseudo-trial rewritten by a third party, there was no "I" who was "confessing" anything . . . Such a gross forgery dealt the *coup de grâce* to what remained of Fonagy's communist ideals, and he began moving heaven and earth to obtain exile in France. I learned a great deal from his important work, especially his observations of language acquisition in children. He noted and described the involvement of the primal urges dependent on the erogenous zones—oral, anal, urethral—in the formation of consonants and vowels. The erotic body impresses itself on the phonemes, flesh speaks, for language is not merely a sign to convey an idea . . .

PS: The instinctual bases of phonation . . .

JK: Exactly! I used those terms and Fonagy's research to analyze the poetry of Stéphane Mallarmé. This great French symbolist is reputed to be an abstruse, ineffable, metaphysical poet. He is undoubtedly all of those things. But Mallarmé is also the author of *Mystery in Literature* and *Music and Letters*, essays in which he avers that it would be possible—and necessary—to revolutionize the alexandrine, the dominant meter of French poetry, by composing and recomposing the musicality embedded in French words—repetition, alliteration, rhythms, and vocalization—to imbue verbal flows with the erotic *vibra-tions* of the speaking body, inseparable from the "message" or "theme" of the poem. We were speaking of Manet earlier: Manet and Mallarmé were linked in terms of their similar esthetics and sensual bent, as well as by Méry de Laurent, the celebrated muse and lover of both . . . Talking of the "instinc-tual bases of phonation," we have only to listen to "Prose for Des Esseintes":

> *Hyperbole! De ma mémoire*
> *Triomphalement ne sais-tu*
> *Te lever, aujourd'hui grimoire*
> *Dans un livre de fer vêtu*[8]

One has to hear the syllables, the consonants and vowels, sense the pronunciation and the energy it unleashes, hear the further meanings carried by the various syllables in a lexi-cal, grammatical chain: *père, bol, phal, ivre, livre, vêtu, veux-tu* [father, bowl, phall, drunk, book, clad, will you] . . . As we listen, the mounting aural polyphony prompts articulation in the mouth, mobilizing tongue and lips and teeth, at the same time as the words spark further meanings and invite us to rev-erie, imagination, creation, in and through this act of reading. After all, the latent theme in "Prose for Des Esseintes" is none other than resurrection.

CF: In fact, one sees how this "inner experience" resides simulta-neously in language and in the body, for both of you. Perhaps you could say something here about *Proust and the Sense of Time.*[9]

JK: Yes, Proust inspired me, in that respect, more immediately than other novelists, with his "involuntary memory" and his revelation of the sadomasochism at the heart of human attachment. And I can't help recalling that prophetic remark of his, so casually thrown out: "Reality, the refuse of experience . . ." Psychoanalysis, if I may come back to it briefly, was just then seeping into linguistics as well, more discreetly and more laboriously, but the field was henceforth open . . . A colleague said something to me just now: "I was a linguist, and you came to our university, and we discussed Chomsky, but we didn't know anything about Freud." Obviously not: "we" were Cartesians, at best. And yet Benveniste had already commented on the place of *language* in Freud's discovery of the unconscious. Benveniste's notion of *enunciation* implied a speaking subject who was not Chomskyan-Cartesian, but alert to phenomenology, to dialogue, and also—more quietly but very clearly, for those with their ear to the ground—in the grip of unconscious instinctual logics.

PS: The body speaks, but most of the time nobody's listening. We don't listen to what our bodies are saying. It's a mistake . . . I'd like to return to something from long ago: what Barthes wrote on the subject of a book of mine called *Event*,[10] dating from 1965. He says this: "*Event* looks back at a golden age, the age of awareness and utterance. Its time is that of the body as it awakens, still brand-new, neutral, untouched by remembrance or signification. Here is the Adamic dream of the total body, marked at the dawn of our modernity by Kierkegaard's cry of 'Give me a body!' The total body is impersonal; identity hovers like a bird of prey high above a slumber in which we peacefully go about our real lives, our true history. As soon as we begin to wake, the bird swoops down, and it is during that dive, before it reaches us, that we must outstrip it and speak. The Sollersian awakening"—sorry, that's how Barthes put it—"is a complex span of time, at once very long and very short. It is a nascent awakening, an awakening that takes its time being born."

The body speaks, and it doesn't speak just anyhow—it has to be deciphered. Here's where analysis comes in, that splendid invention of Freud's, for whom I have the greatest admiration, greater every day in fact, the more I hear people blurting out, in the course of ordinary conversation, enormities of which they seem entirely unaware. I don't wander into Julia's therapy room and say, "So, is it working?" No, I carefully steer clear of psychoanalysts, one is quite enough for me [*laughter*].

CF: Julia, you were saying that Philippe was your best patient.

PS: I am definitely her best patient, and it costs me very dear, actually . . . but it does me so much good, doesn't it?

JK: Apparently it does . . . The most famous patient!

PS: But forget my case, the issue is: What do you get out of your analytical practice?

JK: What do I "get out" of it? I'll tell you. In a book called *New Maladies of the Soul*,[11] I reviewed the recent phenomena my analysands are involved in and exposed to, which are far more difficult to encapsulate than the various forms of totalitarianism: the shifting composition of the family, the new calibrations of sexual difference via the stress on psychological bisexuality, increasingly affirmed by both sexes; narcissistic deficiencies; uncertainties around identity . . . Result? The psychic space itself comes under threat; in some cases, it is almost destroyed. This "inner space" or "psychic interiority" that the West has pinpointed, furthered, and optimized since the time of Narcissus and Plotinus with Christic *prayer* and *confession*, then through the *experience* elucidated by Hegel and Heidegger and also by Georges Bataille, of which

Freud made an observation lab, but also the *lever* empowering a new psychological survival by means of transference/countertransference—well, where are we with *that*? Does *that* continue to protect us from attack, whether internal (biophysiological) or external (the violence meted out by family, society, nature, history)? Or is it on the way out? Since when? Under pressure from the image? From the spectacle? From the slackening of family ties? From the absence of authority? When the dark chamber of the psychic apparatus falls apart, psychosomatic ailments ensue, bouts of depression, vandalism, or addiction, eruptions of the death drive, fanatical outbursts . . . The analyst who hears all this doesn't "get" anything out of it, properly speaking, other than evidence of the need to reevaluate previous knowledge, refine her listening, and find different ways to interpret and accompany this ill-being.

What is in abeyance is the capacity to "psychalize," if you'll forgive the neologism: the ability to put excitation, distress, or trauma into words. To *represent them* by other means too, such as painting, music, dance, sport, but, above all, to name them. Because language not only has the power to displace the upset, by attenuating it, but also to interpret it and ultimately to share it, with the mutual capacity of a partner. In the absence of this modulation, inner space begins to shrink and come undone, and the impulse turns against the source-person, causing them to explode into psychosomatic sickness—if not literally, as a suicide bomber. The human becomes depersonalized until nothing is left but a destructive weapon.

CF: The decomposition-recomposition of the family unit, of fatherhood and motherhood . . .

JK: Yes, motherhood, which feminism has tended to disparage and doesn't easily relate to. "We," the secular democracies, are the only civilization that lacks a discourse on motherhood. There's some sense of what a Jewish mother might be, or a Catholic mother, under the patronage of the Virgin Mary. But the modern mother, often a single mother in the absence of the father or a partner, has nothing to turn to but the super-market and the pediatrician to answer the children's needs and her own anxieties . . . And that, clearly, is not enough for those who end up putting their babies in the freezer . . . Infanticide is hardly a modern invention, it just gets more widely publi-cized by today's mass media. All the same, we shouldn't under-estimate the way contemporary life conditions can aggravate the loneliness of mothers.

But, contrary to a widespread prejudice, psychoanalytic research exists and offers greater support than ever in the face of such phenomena, with better answers than other approaches. For instance, the knowledge of borderline cases and how to treat them, the early monitoring of the mother-baby relationship, the care of autistic children and the interac-tion with other disabilities, from elementary and junior high upward. Psychoanalysis is steeped in these concerns, which I adapt to the analyses undertaken with my adult patients. So I can be in osmosis with their complexity, before fine-tuning the tact of interpretation.

PS: A quick word. The other day, you said, "It's funny, really: peo-ple are exposed to instant information in so-called real time, rushing past at full speed . . . But when it's a question of them-selves, the odd thing is you'd think they lived in a sealed can." Amazing, that, when you come to think of it. To be relentlessly globalized at every second, and yet live stuck inside a can!

Another thing you told me—and I find this more interesting—is that you often struggle to memorize a text . . .

JK: Struggle with the inability to read . . .

PS: I read something, and then I can't remember what it was. Those other people aren't suffering from Alzheimer's, unless it's very early onset, but . . . This is something that absolutely fascinates me, because I believe it to be one of the great symptoms of our time. We could conduct an experiment: I hand out a text of about twenty lines, by whoever you please, Jean-Jacques Rousseau, say; I collect it up after ten minutes, to be generous, and then I ask everybody to tell me what they just read. I'm sure the results would be astounding. I've coined a word for that, the verb *oublire*, which allows me to say to someone who fancies they know me: "I see, *vous m'avez oublu*" [*laughter*].[12] And it's true. You often quote the same complaint from your analysands: I read, but can never concentrate on it, or I can't recall the book I just read. Everyone is assumed to be a reader, to know how to read and all that. I beg to differ. I think that nowadays we're all engaged in a gigantic anti-inner experience.

JK: The people who've "forread" you are caught in Sollersian hate-elove . . . They don't ever appear on my couch. They "forread" you because they approach your writing with a mixture of love and hate. You have a lot of readers, but you never indulge their unhappiness, you challenge it, and they find that hurtful.

PS: Well, so they forread me . . . Hang on a second, that's why I set such store by poetry. In fact, the antidote is surely to learn poems by heart. Defend yourself against every onslaught by learning poetry by heart. Some people do feel that way, though not many: they recite Baudelaire and La Fontaine to themselves . . .

JK: There you're touching on something we haven't sufficiently discussed, we only mentioned it in passing: the role of language, of style, in *experience*. Was it Wittgenstein who said that experience can be shown but not said? Or more precisely, "There is what is inexpressible, and this shows itself, it is the Mystical." "That which can be shown cannot be said." "Clearly, ethics cannot be put into words." He brilliantly defends a *certain* experience. I venture to claim that there are other kinds. In common with the post-Freudians, and the moderns you invited to write in *Tel Quel* and *L'Infini*, magazines that shed considerable light on those thinkers, some of us—including myself, and you too, I believe, in a different way—work on the assumption that *that* can be uttered. Not definitively, or not totally, but it's a part of experience to wager on *that* being sayable. From upstream, in writing, in psychoanalysis . . .

I was looking just now for the famous sentence that preceded us in this wager, the one you comment on in *Dante et la traversée de l'écriture*, if I'm not mistaken. It goes something like this: "He who is ignorant of his language serves idols, and he who sees his language sees God." That's crucial: language as a *link*, a bridge to interpret what is experienced as loss of self, followed by the rebirth of the self. Rebirth of whatever would remain lost in the absence of language: whatever might, without it, be reduced to "talking points" or be stifled by repression or lead to the most barbaric actings out. Psychoanalysis has come to occupy this precise and unexpected place, so as not to leave it to the managerial mercies of politics or institutionalized religion. But instead to reinstate this verbal microcosm in the freedom of the speaking subject, by listening to the unsayable rendered sayable, without end. By restoring it to the experience of subjectivization itself, rather than to any other institution, thus inviting the analysand to locate and live out her singularity. There is little appreciation—or a mistaken one or none—of the degree of transfiguration of freedom, of the human, wrought by psychoanalysis when it is understood like that. Are psychoanalysts themselves aware of it?

PS: What do you think [*laughter*]?

JK: Aside from that, I've also permitted myself to adopt a language that differs from the conceptual idioms of philosophy or theory. While always being a foreigner abroad, and participating in the mixture of languages thrown up by globalization like a rerun of Babel, I've allowed myself that first-person utterance that we call *fiction*.

Why and how did it come about, this authorization? It was all down to you, because you encouraged me from the start . . . Not to write the way you do, since your artistry with and mastery of the language and literary memory of France are completely beyond me, and any attempt to emulate, compete, or genuflect on that terrain would be laughable, to say the least. No, you encouraged me to dress the seizing of experience with my taste for the sensuality that infuses words and the wanderings of the imagination: in short, to dress it in narrative. "*Hagamos cuenta,*" as Teresa of Avila put it: "Let us tell stories, the better to understand." Those words could have been mine. Or again: "I regard it as impossible that love would ever be content to remain stationary."

After that, my personal analysis detached me from conceptual French and enabled me to talk of affects in this second language that became, as a result, ever less foreign. David played a decisive part in my choice of the novel form. Living with a child who's learning French as his birth language means becoming familiar with his "instinctual bases," as taste, smell, touch, and hearing infuse words, grammar, and reasoning. I settled myself in the novel, knowing that, though my works would be unlikely to rival those of Kafka, Proust, Colette, or Sollers, they were nevertheless in equilibrium with the life and death drives, which the dramas of existence never fail to rouse in me; knowing that this equilibrium that I try to "set to music" could be apprehended by the reader, so he could think it, and also feel it, in French. To bring to existence in a *novel* that *inner experience* we've been talking about, fraught with love, reflection, motherhood, commitment, desires—that's what at the present moment seems to me the most desirable, the most difficult, and the most right thing to be doing.

CF: That sensation of exile is very interesting, actually, one can perfectly well feel like an exile or a foreigner without ever stepping out of one's country or language. But with you, Julia, your genuine exile has acted as a stimulus . . .

JK: Could I read out a few lines that have a bearing on foreignness in language? Would it be possible to answer by reading a few pages, later on, toward the end of our conversation?

PS: One is exiled in humanity. There's not a single interesting writer, whether Kafka, Joyce, whoever you care to name, or Mallarmé, or Rimbaud, or others, or Dante, who didn't feel a deep metaphysical banishment by the very fact of being human.

JK: There, that's experience in the strong sense of the word. The verb used by Dante, *trasumanar*, means "to pass though the human" . . . That's the sense in which writing is an experience of exile. Every writer feels it when he wrenches himself out of his so-called normative humanity and innovates, but only Dante formulated it with such absolute concision. Mallarmé says the same thing in another way . . .

PS: They all do, every one of them . . .

JK: Mallarmé, he aspired to write a "total word, new, alien to language". And then Aragon . . .

PS: Every one of them . . .

JK: Aragon confessed to living "in a strange land inside my very land" . . . This poet reinvented the national tongue.

PS: All of these writers dreamed up their salvation, while threatened with being wiped out. Human beings are sleepwalkers, sound asleep, and it's not natural, Pascal thought. Voltaire held the same opinion, really: "They turned devout," he says, "for fear of being nothing." When Manet showed *Olympia* and *The Luncheon on the Grass,* the whole of Paris flocked to spit on and insult his pictures. Manet was taken aback, because, being quite naive, he thought of himself as a producer of the nicest classical painting. He couldn't get over people ganging up to insult him. He died at the age of fifty-one, which is pretty young, after all. He said that sustained abuse crushes you in the long run, makes you lose all taste for life. Ah, that's where inner experience has to be worth its salt, because . . . Would you like to see my insults collection? There's smoke coming out of the computer . . . [*laughter*].

JK: That's your own foreignness in French, and that of many writers. But you push that outsiderness to an extreme that rattles people, because you invite them to an ultimately joyous freedom to *transcend* rather than to *belong.* Which involves a certain solitude, the shunning of massification . . .

I'd like to return to that other foreignness, linked to globalization and overlapping with yours, but not the same as yours. One can be a foreigner in one's own language in order to reawaken it, to restore full potential to it. And one can be a foreigner by being swept up in the flow of hyperconnections, company relocations, globalization. To be caught in the maelstrom of languages, switching from one to the other, is like dying and being reborn, I've said so more than once tonight.

But it can also be a hopelessly painful experience. Some of my students have adopted a foreign language (French on occasion, English by obligation) to apply like a plaster on top of old childhood and family hurts: the foreign language helps them to *forget*, for a while. Then this remedy doesn't pass the test of time, the person sinks into depression before turning up at the hospital of the Cité Universitaire, where I find them somatic or suicidal, because they no longer possess their own words. The newly acquired tongue is no better than a dead skin, a borrowed code that fails to internalize the person's affects. Until it has incorporated the unconscious, it is not a language.

But lately a new human species has emerged, speaking several languages: the new *Homo europeanus*, the Erasmus student—a kaleidoscopic individual who may not completely master all of the twenty-eight tongues, but has a fair grasp of several. And can even play around with them, with a creativity that heralds a startling time to come: the time of federal Europe, something entirely unsuspected by the bulk of depressed Europeans.

PS: We ought to finish on Heidegger's *zeitigt*, "time-making."[13]

JK: Shall we? All right. Fifteen more minutes?

PS: No, ten [*laughter*]!

JK: OK. I was talking about being a foreigner inside language as an allusion to two extracts from past texts of mine . . . The first of these concerns the relationship between French and Bulgarian, the second deals with the experience of death.

It's no use my trying to come back to life in French; for almost fifty years now my French taste has not always been able to resist the jolts of an early music coiled around a memory that is still vigilant. From these connected vessels there emerges a strange language, a stranger to itself, neither from here nor from there, a monstrous intimacy. Like the characters in Proust's refound time, whose long years of voluntary and involuntary memories are embodied in immense spaces, I am a monster of the crossroads.

At the intersection of two languages, and of at least two lengths of time, I mold an idiom that seeks what is obvious so as to hollow out pathetic allusions there and, under the smooth guise of these French words polished like the stone of a holy water font, to uncover the dark gilt of Orthodox icons. Giant or dwarf, the monster who struggles out of them takes pleasure in never being content with itself, at the same time as it exasperates the natives— those of the country of origin as well as those of the receiving country.[14]

And now for a passage taken from *Their Gaze Pierces Our Shadows*, a collection of the letters between myself and Jean Vanier, the Catholic founder of L'Arche, which set up care homes for the disabled in 140 countries, back in 1964. When I arrived in France, as you witnessed, exile put me into the hospital. I got better thanks to you, among others. Here's the text:

I stared at my hands holding the pen, at my face in the mirror. I was not myself, someone else had taken the place of what had been me, I wasn't that other nor was I my previous self, having died in my native language and unsure whether I could survive in the adoptive space of French. Analysis would reconcile me with both those specters, and since then I've existed in French alone, as best I could, not without sporadic auscultation of the still-warm corpse of my mother tongue. But the experience of death, symbolically so intense that it was felt by me as real, took hold inside. When David was born, our early worries could not be named, and we had to behave as though all was well. Until his first coma, two weeks of hanging between life and death, real death this time. A few years later, the same ordeal. I tried to keep going by reading books. And it was on a hospital mattress, at the foot of a hospital cot, that I wrote the pages of my work on Hannah Arendt that examine the difference the philosopher draws between physiological processes and the vital impulse, that is, what the subject and her group have to say and tell about it, and the pages about motherhood as the freedom to begin, the beginning of a singular, ephemeral life, beginning of the self, too, the mother's self-commencement. On both occasions when David came out of his coma, we embarked on a new life, in the grip of that rebirth. Is that a pleasure? Indeed it is, but lined with anguish, softened with serenity, a hope.[15]

CF: Thank you, Julia. A truly beautiful text. Shall we close on that? We'd planned for each of you to say something about the other's books, but it's getting a bit late . . .

PS: One minute . . .

JK: I thought you might discuss the verb *to timeper*,[16] which you used in the context of Bach.

PS: No, no . . . Just a minute. I expect you feel the same as me, and I feel pretty moved. Now, to be moved, in my case, flips at once into the mood that Italian has such a fine word for: *sprezzatura*, "offhandedness."

JK: Here, look . . .

PS: What is it? Oh, how sweet of you . . .

JK: Not really . . . but "being moved," I understand . . . Emotion's tough, it abolishes time, it goes on and on, outside time . . . Anyway, we'd agreed I was to xerox you those pages in large type [*laughter from PS*].

PS: Yes, so this is about time, in Johann Sebastian Bach's *The Well-Tempered Clavier*. If you're agreeable, shall I wind us down in music? Here goes:

Nobody ever says so, but little Bach was a particularly playful, mischievous, cheeky, and fugitive child. Outside of his precocious passion for music and his grave demeanor in church, he was always to be seen scampering about the countryside in the vicinity of Eisenach. Who had never watched him as he raced, scurried, swooped, stopped dead, dashed forward again like the clappers, fell back on the grass with arms outflung, sprang up, and ran headlong till running out of breath, when he would sit down and have a long think before resuming his antics, to the despair of his mother, who could make no sense of his way of tempering, or more exactly *timepering*, regulating the tempest, and that awful crucifixion business. To resuscitate the spirals, that's the journey. And that is just what darkens the countenance of the Prussian king one day when the aged Bach shows up. Everyone is in the dining room. A footman enters, whispers to the king. He stands up and says: "Gentlemen, old Bach has arrived." So everybody stands up, since the king stood up. They don't care, of course: old Bach will be sat before the keyboard. Nobody wonders if he's had supper. He traveled through driving snow, and he's got to perform, he didn't come here to eat. That's what darkens the countenance of the king: old Bach's dizzy, childish joy for all to see, Bach on whom time shall have no dominion, his uninterrupted prayer, his movement of perpetual adoration, in short, his love.[17]

That's all, folks.[18]

CF: So we'll bring this encounter to an end on that word: *love*.

3

CHILDHOOD AND YOUTH
OF A FRENCH WRITER

MANY THANKS to all of you here for joining us in this encounter with the childhood and youth of a French writer, Philippe Sollers.

After so many years of sharing my life with him, it is as a lover, a wife, a mother, a writer, a psychoanalyst, and a literary theorist that I address you today. Antoine Guggenheim has suggested as much, with discreet precision, and I reiterate it in my turn because I perceive the intensity of your attentive presence.

I will not duck this intensity. My response is simply that if this cohabitation of our two foreignnesses—Sollers's and mine—continues to defy time, it's because *it writes itself* in different registers and with a mutual resonance. Since I situate our "joint pact" in the logic of "writing itself," I might have declined the invitation I received to present the "childhood and youth of a French writer, Philippe Sollers." I accepted, partly because the Bernardins monastery space places writing at the horizon of the Incarnation, and I regard the incommensurable intimacy of the experience of writing as precisely that, an incarnation—worlds away from the "celebrity" culture exhibited in what are currently known as "talking points." But I am here above all because I feel very strongly that the themes of this encounter—childhood, youth, writing, Frenchness—are far from being transparent, let alone natural, topics. Instead they grow ever more unfathomable and even shocking amid the banality of mind that threatens us and is, in my view, the radical ailment of the day.

"A French writer," indeed "the most French of French writers": that's how Philippe Sollers appeared to the student I was when we met, soon after my arrival in this country from my native Bulgaria. And this impression has been confirmed and deepened all through the evolution of his work, from *The Park, Laws, H,* and *Paradise* to *The Taste War, A Divine Life, Watteau in Venice, A True Novel,* and *Perfect Discourse.*[1] The truth is, he who was once dubbed "Diderot's nephew"[2]—the same Sollers—is "incorrigibly French" in the broadest sense, derived from the eighteenth century and that signally French way of thinking in novels. When I say "novel" it's the French kind I think of, as full of talking as of romancing, teeming with monologues and dialogues in the tradition of Voltaire and Stendhal, in which curiosity along with a cheerful, encyclopedic vivacity infect the reader with a taste for Rabelais, Molière, and Watteau, for Manet, Fragonard, Cézanne, and Picasso, for Artaud and Van Gogh, Mozart and Nietzsche, Freud and Joyce, Courbet and Céline. A novel as French as the port of Bordeaux—that *bord de l'eau*, water's edge, evoking Venice while opening toward England, where the first French Parlement voted for the emancipation of the Jews . . . Not that this should make us overlook the yellow stars that reappeared there under the Nazi occupation.

It's understood that, with Sollers, "French" is to be taken in the sense in which "national identity"—as constructed by great literature, and, more than any other, by great French literature—serves as the most effective of antidepressants. Why? Because in the experience of literature, the experience of a necessarily sensitive language and an inevitably historic narrative, French history has fashioned an equivalent to the sacred that is unique in the world. All peoples have literatures, but only in France does literature rival the sacred on the level of *experience*, because it has successfully shown that identity (personal, sexual, and also national) is not a cult so much as an interrogation, a perpetual querying that is forever, precisely, being written.

Against those who uphold national identity as a bulwark against the "others," migrants in particular; against those who refuse to acknowledge the importance of identity because they lack the courage to see it through to the other side reflectively, the French writer that is Philippe Sollers wages his "taste war" in a country which is that of the French language as it took shape throughout the history of this people, and particularly through the diversity of French writers.

I've actually been told, on the other side of the Atlantic, that Sollers is *too French*.[3] It is bad form these days to use the adjective *French*, because apparently it sounds nationalistic. Some people might define themselves at most as "Francophone," which has a more cosmopolitan ring, despite the postcolonial, victimized undertone, but, too bad, it'll do for highlighting the inherent culpability of being French. There's nothing of the sort in Philippe Sollers, the author of *French Follies*.[4]

Nothing of the sort in you. The child and adolescent from Bordeaux—a place you fondly revisit in your novels and essays—is always sublimating, from inside and out, recollection both recent and ancient. And also this current France, the land whose verbal musicality and physical fiber you embody, the better to laugh and cry over it. You proceed, of course, in the company of the most illustrious sons of Bordeaux, from Montaigne, La Boétie, and Montesquieu down to Mauriac, including a galaxy of special favorites: Pascal, Saint-Simon, Sade, Lautréamont, Rimbaud, André Breton, Georges Bataille, Paul Morand, Sartre, and not forgetting women like Mme de Sévigné or even Beauvoir . . .

That style of Frenchness, no solemn cult but a matter of questions, tastes, thoughts, and shouts of laughter, is the one you practice, and it's the one I fell for, as our audience will have guessed. This French vision, this French writing—in the sense in which writing is a destiny and a project—are just what is lacking, surely, from the contemporary social contract in its hunt for an elusive refoundation. What if the foundation being sought were to consist of this very taste for imbibing, by embodying it, political and literary memory, literary and political memory? What if this were the great means of engineering its rebirth, its ceaseless reincarnation in the reinvention of its vital force?

In times as dire as these, opting to wage a war of taste against and within national identity, through the memory of the nation's tongue, literature, and political history, may seem outrageous, and in fact it is. How is it even possible? When I read your work, I seem to hear you telling us: The reason it's possible is because I've kept my childhood and youth alive inside me. Unless it's because you conduct your writing like a relentless war of taste against each and every identity, posture, pose, value, dogma, platitude, absolute, and the rest, so that your readers don't register your foreignness as an anguished wail from some totalitarian catastrophe, nor as a confession of personal distress, nor indeed as a protest against social or racial exclusion—all these themes being the toast of the publishing market. No, your particular foreignness, irksome singularity that dictates your recasting of the French language, comes through to us as the outsiderhood of perpetual infancy and youth. But what infancy? What youth? The childish state you make us read and fathom is—unsurprisingly—nothing like the divine innocence of the Infant Jesus, nor does it have the inborn purity of Rousseau's children. Closer to the Freudian image, the figure of the child in your books transmits the fullness of sensation, sorrow, pleasure, or sickness with a classical clarity overlapping with the hallucinatory and the poetic; this stretches from the flavors of Bordeaux to the secrets of your characters, portrayed as feeling concepts, rather like the men and women of that southwest France in which Hölderlin glimpsed the perpetuation of the Greek miracle.[5] Could the infant Sollers be a lab researcher who prefigures the avid curiosity of the pseudonymous writer? A sort of Odysseus, whom Homer describes as *polytropos*, "the man of twists and turns";[6] in Latin *sollers*, *sollertis*—the wily, the adroit, the elusive one?

As for the adolescent, he helps me to better understand the teens who come to my consulting room. The teenage Sollers is a believer—fittingly for this venue, the Bernardins. Embarked as he is on a quest for his political, amorous, and psychic ideals, and unshakably convinced of the existence of Heaven, he can't be anything except at war.

The teenage Sollers is a believer in revolt who can't stop reinventing his own Heaven. Adam and Eve were adolescents, as were Dante and Beatrice; we are all adolescents when we're in love.[7]

As an admirer of Baudelaire, you could well have said, echoing the author of the *Flowers of Evil*: "Genius is but childhood clearly expressed"[8] or, more simply, as Lamartine put it: "Yes, to you I return, cradle of my childhood."[9] But you don't say that, because you don't "return" to that cradle, properly speaking ("Genius is nothing more nor less than childhood recovered at will":[10] Baudelaire again—it goes for Rimbaud as reread by Bataille, but it doesn't apply to you). Nor do you evince the voluptuous desolation of Marcel Proust in his remembrance of things past. Let alone the "suffering" of Bernanos, who, "once childhood was behind him," struggled "for a long time" to reach "at the far end of night . . . a different dawn."[11] On the contrary, you go through childhood without ever leaving it, like the Daoist sage who claimed to be the only one feeding from the mother.[12] Because you lift childhood and youth into the present moment, right here, today.

You relive them in writing, here and now. How do you do that? The answer couldn't be plainer, it's like the purloined letter in Poe's story. The theme is so ubiquitous in your novels that people would rather censor it; it never occurs to them that the ease with which childhood and adolescence are sustained in your rewriting of identities, especially French identity, could be due to that. The "purloined letter" is the bond with women and with mothers, intimate and rebellious at once, cultivated by the narrator of your novel *Women*.[13] The constant curiosity that moves you arises from your curiosity toward the opposite sex, and that's the one that radiates to infinity across Being and History. Insatiable curiosity, for where "the great seriousness at last begins, the true question mark is at last set down" (as Nietzsche has it).[14] That question mark crystallizes in your laugh, so serious that it sounds anxious, unless this is a respectful revolt or perhaps an incredulous one. And since nobody is quite as guarded as the person who seems to give himself away to everyone, your media-savvy mask—on top of that laugh—shields the invisible solitude of a heart as uncompromising as it is gleeful. Leading the narrator of *A Divine Life* to behave precisely like an alter ego of Nietzsche.[15]

One of the high points in this interrogation of the greatly serious occurred in our real lives, for a change: when you read from

Meister Eckhart over your father's grave, in the cemetery of Bordeaux. That event cast surprising light on your own interrogation, the way you unpick the son's relationship to the father by means of writing: a crucial question, which Antoine Guggenheim has forcefully articulated from the standpoint of a theologian who reads your work.

I'll stop here with my canvas of hypotheses. I've selected some passages from *A True Novel: Memoirs*,[16] which I now invite you, Philippe, to read and comment on.

4

LOVE OF THE OTHER

BERNADETTE BRICOUT: To introduce Julia Kristeva and Philippe Sollers is a challenge. I don't much like labels, and, in any case, they both exceed all the definitions in which one could try to pigeonhole them. They have never ceased to overstep their own borders. They are beings in motion. Perhaps only a baroque painter might be able to capture them in the swing of that motion.

Julia Kristeva is a writer, psychoanalyst, and semiologist, professor emeritus at the University of Paris-7 Diderot, where I am the vice president in charge of cultural life and the university in the city. Julia Kristeva is doctor *honoris causa* at several universities abroad, a list to which the most recent addition is Haifa, Israel, where she was awarded that distinction on May 27, 2014. In 2004 she was the first laureate of the Holberg Prize, an equivalent to the Nobel Prize in the field of human sciences. She received the Hannah Arendt Prize in 2006 and the Václav Havel Prize in 2008. She defines herself as a "European citizen of Bulgarian origin, French nationality, and American adoption"—a cosmopolitan intellectual, in short. The best image for her trajectory is that of crossing frontiers, between countries, cultures, disciplines, and genres. Her motto? "I travel myself." She is on her way.

The oeuvre of Philippe Sollers is well known: subversive, shimmering, nuanced, profuse, and veined with impudent elegance. On a worldlier level, let us recall that Philippe was born in Bordeaux, that he founded the magazine *Tel Quel* and its publishing arm in 1960, and then the magazine and publishers *L'Infini* in 1983; that he is the author of more than sixty books, a magazine director, an editor, an unearther of talents, and an insatiable reader. Philippe Sollers often muses on his singular "experience of limits" with regard to the words of the French language, apt to be buried under a flood of misunderstandings when writing, which is life, thinks its way through history and the passions in novelistic form. Among those words smothered by misunderstandings, the word *love* stands out. It is at once an insistently present word in contemporary society and a much abused one, since we live in a culture where sex is no longer an art but a technique, where encounters are often programmed on specialized websites, Prince Charming and his princess surfing the Internet in search of each other. They will recognize their mate according to compatibilities of age, weight, and height, to social criteria and financial standards; in no time they will be sharing their most intimate feelings with us in a television studio. And yet love, as we know, demands secrecy. This unstable object, this fragile thing, this dimly contoured thing is what we are going to explore tonight, with the help of woven words that will obey no preordained design. We have not conferred beforehand.

Julia Kristeva, on April 28, 2011, during our Festival of Enlightenment, you gave one of the "Encyclopedic Consultations," entitled "Talk to Me of Love." You spoke about love and the special place it occupies in your life, in our lives, in literature, in psychoanalysis. Tonight we are going to talk of love again. Philippe and Julia are a couple. We haven't pronounced the word *Joyaux* [Jewels], that is, your real married name, but in all due secrecy and with all the discretion to which we are so attached, it's true that there is a jewel in the story of this couple. We might be led to talk about it in retrospect, since one always talks about love in retrospect.

JULIA KRISTEVA: Yes. If I'm not mistaken, Bernadette, you're giving me the floor. I thought earlier that Philippe Sollers, who is more at home in French and in matters of love than I am, might be the one to begin. But he decided . . . Is there a problem?

BB: Just between us, he said that if I gave him the floor, he would hand it straight back to you. We were trying to avoid that . . .

JK: Courtesy and parity *oblige*; I shall therefore sacrifice myself [*laughter*]. First of all, I thank the Cercle Bernard-Lazare for hosting this event and I thank you, ladies and gentlemen, for coming along to listen to us this evening. It's a hard test, for sure, to speak of love, because the subject eludes definition, as you just pointed out, Bernadette; so let me thank you as well, or you above all, for accepting the responsibility of introducing us and steering our exchanges. Love has not remained unchanged through the history that has stamped us, and it also varies over the course of our personal history. I presume you planned for me to speak first because I could be relied on to provide a general, brainy overview, and then the playfulness—there's no avoiding play in love, is there?—might come into its own with the intervention of Philippe Sollers. Well, as it happens, I'd like to sidestep synthesis and solemnity, with the help of two dodges.

The first involves the feminine genius, supposedly expert on matters of love. Of the three women whose portraits I've sketched (Hannah Arendt, Melanie Klein, and Colette), Colette—the most renowned for "those delights so carelessly described as physical"—is also the one who didn't like the word *love*. "That uninflected word," she wrote, "is not enough for me." She goes on to cite a "trans-Pyrenean philosopher" who only ever used one word for any negative experience or thing: *filth*. In the same way, she in substance went on, some people are so incapable of nuance that "they only have one word for 'love,' which is equally absurd." So she vowed to avoid using that word, that "good fat love," because the experience of love can only be conveyed through metaphors and stories. The depressive, jealous young woman of the early years in Paris, saddled with her fickle husband Willy, became a writer; she narrated Claudine's life and her own, the dawning of the day, the pure and the impure, right down to the very fabric of the world composed of erotic shivers, flowers and animals, nudity and spells . . . And always love, directly and indirectly, as far as it'll go.

I faced up in my own way to this perilous definition, this improbable encapsulation, by writing *Tales of Love*:[1] a book that intermingled the stories I was hearing from my patients, their accounts of obviously unbearable situations, with the metamorphoses undergone by the emotion of love in Western culture. Beginning with Plato's *Symposium*, the priestess Diotima and the maze of homosexual affects that led to a universal philosophy of Goodness and Beauty, and moving on of course to the Song of Songs, my favorite text about being *in love*, which ushered in—for the first time anywhere, I believe—the possibility of a man and a woman being *in love*. Pure poetry, braided into a philosophy of the impossible and bursting with joy, even so. To me, the most fascinating thing about the Song is that, although many scholars agree that the author was King Solomon, it is the woman who is shown theatrically exulting in her love of their love. For the first time in history, the voice of a woman in love is heard! The *amorous discourse* in Judaism, and for all who are attentive to its message, is the work of *a woman in love*.

The Christian experience—"God is love," "In the beginning was love,"—clearly takes up and develops this nuptial song, by way of an astonishing investigation into the bond of love, which is at once physical and rhetorical. While discouraging-cum-purifying the yearnings of the flesh, it comes up with a host of psychological subtleties and stylistic acrobatics. Henceforward love excels at languages and the arts; they become inextricable. And, as Catholic mysticism elevates the paradoxes of love (Everything-love, Nothing-love, Being-love, Void-love), the vocabulary of philosophy is forged and the way is prepared for baroque art.

The history of European civilization and its dissemination on other continents modulate this amatory idiom, diversify and propagate it: there's courtly love, romantic love, Stendhal's love in red and black, the *amour fou* of the surrealists, Artaud's love in smithereens, Bataille's incestuous love, and Joyce's ironic Greco-Judeo-Christian love, the same as that hidden in the chuckle of Sollers's concise French . . . Love leads us into a tireless investigation of language, and I ask you to consider that love only abides, only exists, by virtue of our capacity to strain toward the telling of this unfathomable, unnameable back and forth *between two*.

And the present? Modern life has trivialized *hard sex*,[2] which is not to say that it has altogether cleared it of guilt; around back rooms and S&M sessions, neurosis carries on undeterred, embedded in orgies, encysted into the lining of "sexual liberation." Perhaps love can be found within "values" or what remains of them? But where are they? At the summit of the state? In the zeal of spiritual souls, themselves outflanked by fundamentalists and assorted fanatics? Love finds refuge in hidden complicities and in families, whatever else you may say about them, and it cohabits with hate, which a dash of affection, lightheartedness, and, most definitely, childhood can still salvage from disaster. Modernity's luck turned up in the person of an atheist Jew, Dr. Sigmund Freud, who "discovered the unconscious," or so the books tell us. But what did he really discover? That God is in the unconscious and hell as well? Theologians knew that already. That all men are babies, and women too, but somewhat less? Mothers have known that since time immemorial. The Viennese neuropsychiatrist discovered that unhappiness is a love blocked, in waiting. So he put it on the couch. Tell me what ails you; you will be addressing a discourse of love to me, but you don't have to know that. Pain-love, failure-love, will be transformed into therapy by your remembered stories. It won't heal you, in the strict sense, but it will truly make you feel better: new projects, new encounters . . .

I'm there now: my meeting with Philippe.

The date is May 1966, Europe is still cut in two by the iron curtain, I am a research fellow in Sofia and preparing my doctoral thesis on the French "nouveau roman." General de Gaulle, who can already see Europe stretching from the Atlantic to the Urals, hands out grants to young people from Eastern Europe who speak French. But the communist government of Bulgaria only gives them to old people who don't speak French. Result: nobody leaves.

Just before Christmas 1965, as the director of the literature institute had gone up to Moscow, my thesis supervisor advised me to apply to the cultural service at the French embassy. My parents had had the excellent notion of making me learn French, ever since kindergarten with the Dominican nuns, and my studies in Romance philology and the thesis topic impressed the cultural attaché: I could leave right away. I *had* to leave right away, before the director of the institute came back and foreseeably stopped me. The grant would only arrive at the end of January, my father could only come up with five dollars, and a friend would be waiting for me at Le Bourget—but he never showed . . . I've often told this story, you'll find it in my novel, *The Samurai*.[3]

I got to Paris on Christmas Eve; it was snowing; the French didn't have a clue about snowplows; they still don't; my thin boots let water in; the Parisians weren't dressed the way they are in the (rare) copies of *Elle* and *Vogue* that ever made it to the Alliance Française, and I had no ticket home . . . Regardless, I went straight to the lectures given by Roland Barthes and then signed up for more with Gérard Genette. They explained to me that the "nouveau roman" had been supplanted by the "nouveau 'nouveau roman,'" and that I absolutely must meet the top practitioner in that genre, Philippe Sollers. I'd never heard the name before, so I rushed to the national library in rue de Richelieu and looked up the last issue of *Clarté* (the Communist Youth magazine). There I found the photograph in profile of a most awesome young man, given that he set out in just one page how, in order to change a society, you first had to change its language. The surrealists and the Russian futurists (Mayakovsky, Khlebnikov, and the linguist Jakobson himself) had already put forward that idea, but I hadn't expected to see it expounded all over again in French, and with such stylish aplomb. I asked him for an interview. He welcomed me in his small office at the Seuil publishing house. He was as handsome, if not handsomer, than in the photo, the antithesis of your typical writer, a skinny, stammering sort as a rule; he had the confident swagger of a soccer player. And to cap it all, here was someone who seemed to listen, who took an interest in my reading, in cultural life such as it is in a communist country . . . You have to remember the context of the time: France had just emerged from the Algerian war, everyone seemed so cagey—Christmas, wrapped gifts, the crowds in the big stores, Christmas mass in Notre-Dame, nobody looking at anybody else, and suddenly I meet this lively, genial writer . . . We stuck together from then on, he took me to the Île de Ré and introduced me to his family, and our encounter carries on: every day a fresh encounter. That's about it . . .

BB: For you, Philippe, the encounter—your meeting Julia—falls under the sign of what Jean Rousset termed a "decisive revelation." It was an earthquake. An endlessly reinvented discovery, a slow crystallization. All of that simultaneously, I imagine? Tell us something about it.

PHILIPPE SOLLERS: In the office where I used to receive the writers and thinkers of the day, who do I see come in but a young woman of twenty-five, perfectly gorgeous, who claims to be a student from Bulgaria [*laughter*]. Well, now, have a seat, what's your business? And though she's a student, I find that she speaks impeccable French, with a faint accent that is sadly on the way out now, but was very musical and charming. I hold on to my cool . . . [*laughter*]. Later, but not immediately: there was no instant bid for appropriation. So, me keeping my cool, as I said; I'm listening and then I think: she's about to ask me all kinds of trite studenty questions; it's going to be a pain; college students are there to be manipulated, infiltrated, subverted, but this one being from Bulgaria, on a student grant, very sweet I'm sure, but then again she's going to ask me all those idiotic questions, French-type questions. Give me a break . . . But suddenly (smart of her!) she starts on stuff I know something about, but not much, such as the Russian futurists, poets like Mayakovsky, people who back then were eliminated by Stalinism to make way for the monumental stupidity of socialist realism—you know the kind of thing, paintings of tractors and Picasso as decadent artist. So I'm listening with the greatest interest and thinking to myself, hey, at last someone with a different perspective or a different experience than everyone else. Naturally she brings up that great linguist Roman Jakobson—who we met later; he became a friend of ours—and I say to myself: Ah, remarkable scope, this girl is really very interesting, not only extremely pretty but highly intelligent to boot, so I'm going to ask her out to dinner [*laughter*]. Do you see? It's what they call a *coup de foudre*, a lightning strike, but this one struck quickly and for keeps: like you meet someone and you know straightaway that it's going to last. It was a weird feeling, because there are strikes that have faded away by morning and nocturnal strikes that are not necessarily of lightning. So something else must be going on. And sure enough we went to dinner, to La Coupole—a different place in those days—and it's true to say we fairly stuck together after that. Did I kiss her that night, at Duroc metro station? I tried to. And she, very cleverly, because she's a great chess player, in life as with her patients and in every way; she hung back awhile, to drive the pressure up, and that's how a pretty major event finally took place.

The first thing I noticed about Julia is that she was at once identified as a foreigner. Now, let me tell you what love is: love of the other, which happens to be the name for it tonight; something that develops very quickly in certain individuals, inasmuch as they feel alien not only to themselves but aliens in their country and as their very identity. If you don't feel foreign yourself, you'll never meet a person from abroad, not even if they live next door. In my case, for biographical reasons, I felt like a "stranger" from the start, which reminds me of the title of a splendid book of Julia's, *Strangers to Ourselves*,[4] posing the question about identity, because "I is another," as Rimbaud said. If one hasn't felt that way from early on, owing to language, to a bunch of experiences and so forth, one has absolutely no chance of escaping those prejudices and clichés that are historically so overwhelming and, by the way, have come back with a vengeance, as you'll have noticed. It's also a matter of politics, and one has to be aware, where that's concerned, of the foreignness one carries inside. If I hadn't been possessed by that fundamental feeling of foreignness, I'd never have become close to a strange foreigner. Roland Barthes published a splendid text in defense of Julia, during a period when she'd come under attack, called "The Foreign Woman,"[5] which defines all that, all those xenophobic prejudices of the French. Plus, a woman who actually *thinks*, beware! So, episode one: the far-right press basically accuses her of being a special envoy of Soviet espionage—yes, pretty dumb, thank you very much; but what's worse is that she falls sick. She has a Bulgarian passport, a hammer and sickle passport. We wait in Accident and Emergency together, at the Cochin Hospital, and it turns out there's no room to put her in; she's out in the corridor because, you know: "Who's this person? Where's she from? Do *you* know where she's from?" Etc. We got married for thoroughly practical reasons, to be honest, because she was already getting offers from the United States; she'd fast been spotted as a brilliant scholar. Enough about that. "Honoris causa," that's her nickname at home, she's honoris causa here and honoris causa there [*laughter*], there's no end to it; she's honoris causa in Haifa—what do the people demand? I can answer that: Julia Honoris Causa. I'm a traitor to my social class; I've deprived my lady suitors of a highly eligible chap, hence my dreadful reputation, no need to look any farther. Worse, I hail from an Anglophile bourgeois family who listened to the broadcasts of Radio Londres in 1940, "The French talking to the French, here are some personal messages . . ." Our first floor was occupied by the Germans we listened to Radio Londres in the attic, and in the cellar we hid the English airmen who had to be smuggled into Spain. Foreignness, foreignness . . .

BB: A seminal encounter . . .

PS: Together we fell into a dialogue that never stopped, we are still deep into a conversation with no end in sight, because it's full of arguments; though we don't always see eye to eye, the intensity of the conversation never flags. It was a physical *coup de foudre* without a doubt, but also an intellectual one—the two combined; I'd wish for everyone to experience the same thing, the essential encounter, really. So, regarding "love of the other," what it means is that I expected the other—and still expect the other who is myself—to surprise me. That's what keeps us together, more connected than ever, I'd say, for other reasons that have to do with each of our lives.

BB: Thank you for those reminiscences. There's an African proverb that goes: "The rope that could tie up thoughts has not yet been woven." The same goes for people.

PS: We were married on August 2, 1967, which makes it, let's work it out . . .

BB: When you reach fifty years, it'll be your golden anniversary!

PS: Gold is good, but diamond will be better, since we're also called *Joyaux*. Philippe Joyaux, Julia Joyaux, and our son, David Joyaux. Which doesn't prevent Kristeva and Sollers: the whole range.

BB: Your commitment to the long haul is unusual. We live in societies that prize the moment, the immediate, the urgency of each encounter.

PS: We didn't meet online, that's for sure [*laughter*].

BB: So there's a commitment to the enduring. But this commitment does not entail, as far as you both are concerned, a "fusion" of the couple.

PS: Fusion? One of the two always winds up as the victim. No good. This is something we've actively thought about, of course. I always come back to the Chinese yin and yang: unlike what the West has always imagined, two people are not supposed to merge into one. Metaphysically, for the West, union means fusion. Whereas, from the Chinese point of view, as soon as you have two, you have four. How? Her feminine side will never be the same as mine; my masculine side will never equate to hers, so that makes four of us. A two-way dialogue in which respectful, loving parity between the two consists of knowing they're a foursome.

Any meeting is first and foremost the collision of one childhood with another. Her childhood interests me, since we were born in such different countries. I ought to learn her language, but she is absolutely extraordinary in her understanding of mine. She comes from a damaged, tragic part of the world, witness the death of her father; she wrote a beautiful

book about that, actually, *The Old Man and the Wolves*.[6] It dealt
with the totalitarian, Stalinist regime of the time . . . How can
one become solidary with a childhood that wasn't in the least
bit shared, except by holding on to the ways of childhood? We
two act like kids together, we communicate like kids: I make
her laugh a lot, for example. You wouldn't think so, but she can
laugh her head off . . . I make her laugh, and she makes me
scared when it's called for, and so on. We play hide-and-seek
in this relationship, like children. Here's a possible definition
of love: you only love someone when you recognize the child
in yourself and in the other, for the other.

JK: The role of foreignness and how it keeps us together, and
how our relationship lasts because we are not two people, but
four. OK!

The romantic notion of couplehood hankers after osmosis,
after fusion. It's a charming, adolescent, fabulous idea: everyone loves a fairy tale, and I'm no exception, but I make fun
of the clichés stuck fast to my eternal damsel's skin—I often
hum that Marilyn Monroe number, "I'm incurably romantic,"
to entertain Philippe and our son David, who don't actually
believe a word: they think I'm all Doctor Honoris Causa. In
the heat of passion, during orgasm, when the lovers project
themselves into time and into death, fusion really does occur.
It is ek-static: love and death, exuberant draining of ener-
gies and identities, "I am the other," fusion and confusion of
the man and the woman. Freud affirmed that only genital-
ity "breaks through group ties," and this acme of the "primal
scene" is also the apogee of freedom, at once a mighty antide-
pressant and the occasion of greatest fragility. In parallel, the
endurance of the couple in time is a permanent composition, in
the musical sense, implying the tact necessary for recognizing

the foreignness of the other and the self and allowing that to flourish. Not swallowing up the other in a pseudofusion that ultimately proves to be dominated by the narcissism of one partner alone, either the man or the woman, but continuing to construct the difference, and even the foreignness, of the partner. His strangeness—his oddities—can be disconcerting and annoying; I get mad sometimes, I show it, I let it out—a little, not too much—tactfully, because one can't always be in harmony, and storms are part of the encounter. But the atmosphere clears as our deep-seated affinity sorts out any discord, and the rhythm of the composition resumes.

BB: A composition . . .

JK: That emotional and intellectual attunement between us struck me at once—we both felt it, I think. We found so much to say, to share, to learn . . . For it wasn't just the marquis de Sade profile and the sporty legs that seduced me. It was even more, perhaps, or certainly just as much, the speed at which you used to read, and still do . . . The first book we read together, in bed in your study at Le Martray, was Nietzsche's *Beyond Good and Evil*: I was still on the first paragraph when you were turning the page . . . And saying to me, "You don't weigh anything, how strange, a body with no weight." What could a young Bulgarian student from Sliven have in common with you, you with the left-wing Catholic family you mentioned just now, your schooling at the Lycée Montaigne, then with the Jesuits; a survivor of the Algerian War where your friends lost their lives, then Mauriac–Aragon–Le Seuil, a Médicis Prize, "the beloved of his fairies" (the words are Breton's), and all the rest of it. You who transcended asthma and other frail-little-boy illnesses by throwing yourself headlong into rugby and soccer . . .

PS: As a very decent right-winger . . .

BB: Philippe reminds me more of a Roman emperor!

JK: The Roman look is glaring: my sister used to call you Justinian, remember? Me, I'll settle for those Zidane muscles.

PS: That's a bit much!

JK: What do you mean, he's the best! Our son goes: "Zizou" . . .

I was talking about our irreconcilable, but sharable, forms of foreignness. The son of Bordeaux, and proud of it, that you were, along with your Bordeaux family—they, admittedly, after some minor qualms—made me generously welcome. Exile continued to be a trial, of course. I am addressing an audience who knows about exile and knows that this tragedy can also be a stroke of luck. Because the rejection, the exclusion, the sense of being an intruder or usurper imposed on us by the "entitled," those who "belong by rights," push us to the margins: we're not "one of them." And from that boundary a critical gaze is possible, the freest of all gazes in that it's detached from the *belonging* assumed to be normal and natural. Provided, of course, one doesn't fall into the cult of "origins," wallowing in nostalgia for some long-lost "native homeland" . . . Only then does foreignness become a necessary condition for independent thought. "The thinking life is an outsider's life," said the Greeks, echoed by Hannah Arendt, and Proust anticipated her by including among the "outsiders" homosexuals, artist, and writers . . .

Of course, for each one of you, for each of us, there will be different reasons for the pain inflicted by exile and for the reversal of that pain into liberty of thought. For my part, the metamorphosis that I'm sounding out with you here is owed, firstly, to the person of Philippe, who incessantly writes his own foreignness, but also to his family, and to my own family, whom I don't forget, and who surrounded me with love. This "portmanteau" word should here be understood as a *linkage* that instills in the child the indispensable *trust* that I call the "need to believe": the foundation and condition of the "desire to know," which is then in a position to scrutinize the "belief" to the point of abolishing it if need be. In this way, given that I *believe*—in the sense of an impregnable certainty—that I am loved, that Dad loves me, say, that Mom loves me, well, then, not even jealousy has the power to poison me. So-and-so doesn't love me, he prefers someone else, a rival or rivals, competition muddying my path? So what, he's wrong! I don't care!

PS: Or she's wrong . . .

JK: Or she, of course. She, my sister, my mother. Such prototypes of my relationships with women taught me to respect difference on this terrain, too, to recognize my deficiencies, but also to place my bets on solidarity and devotion or, may I say, the gift of self? My sister was a brilliant violinist, a student of Oistrakh's at the Moscow Conservatory. Whereas I, alas, while adoring music and admiring her artistry, couldn't sing a note. It never once occurred to me to get upset about that failing. To each their kingdom, their uniqueness. Was it my mother's capacity to give herself to her two daughters, to her husband, her family, that impressed on me the value of *giving*, intrinsic to love, and superior to excellence?

One day there was a game on Bulgarian radio; you had to answer the question: "What is the fastest form of transportation in the world?" and send in your reply with an illustrative drawing. "A plane," said my little sister. "A rocket," I corrected. "Thought," was our mother's answer. I was at the age when girls try to act like cheeky boys, so I retorted smugly: "That doesn't work, you can't draw thoughts!" Mom was very good at drawing. With a few strokes of the pencil she sketched a snowman with a droopy head—the snow was melting under a sunbeam—being orbited by a Sputnik released from a rocket. "Man may die, yet his thought conquers the Universe." We sent in the answer and the drawing . . . under my name. I won. For my mother, this devotion was simply normal: it wasn't any kind of sacrifice, nothing but the transmission of the gift of self. We transcend ourselves together; you can receive without fear of losing your way; thought belongs to women, too, moves between women, yin or yang; it'll never melt; we are part of it, co-present for evermore.

I think back to that incident whenever, in our couple or family life, love becomes care. The loved one is never an "object of care"; he or she provides it along with me.

BB: It's about concern for the other.

JK: Concern for the childlike part of the other, which prompts me as a woman—wife or mother—to identify with this infant state, its avidity, its distress, its desire for an ideal performance. I participate in that alchemy; I shadow the impulse; I turn into a tot or a teen myself. All of the temporal phases of life are telescoped, revoked, suspended in that instant of . . . of love, if we still want to use that unwieldy word. But such an enigmatic, such a singular instant . . . No, it can't be turned into a model or held up as a pattern, certainly not! It makes me think of that outside-time that maybe I encounter in the transference-countertransference process, which then becomes communicable . . .

BB: Exactly. In *Treasure of Love*—I adore that title, dear Philippe—you write with reference to Stendhal: "Love is like finding a relative who had passed away. His gaze pierces through death, and around him teems a wealth of vivid details: shapes, sounds, colors, scents. Love is born of life being written."[7] And what we glimpse in Julia's very beautiful, very rich contribution, especially toward the end, is the thread linking love and creativity. So maybe we'll go back to the theme of love in analysis, since every love story is written on the couch . . . Well, that's not how *you* write it, Philippe. A psychoanalyst knows that all stories come down to talking about love, but: "Love is born of life being written." When you were twenty-one, you wrote in *A Strange Solitude*: "When we are very young we want love to have an ambiguous, unfamiliar character, as if derived from a magical tradition."[8] Once again we're in the land of childhood. I'd like you to say more about the link between love and creativity.

PS: One of the best photos I've ever seen of Julia is of her as a baby [*laughter*]. Sometimes you have to go find the little girl in a woman. Which is a lot harder than it might seem, because it's really a matter of stealing her away from her mother. The Song of Songs says that love is as powerful as death. That's quite something: so if I feel love, am I going to be as powerful as death, or maybe overcome death?

Stendhal wrote the following amazing sentence, casually, just like that: "Love has always been the greatest concern of my life, or rather, the sole concern." You know his epitaph, which he wrote in Italian: "He lived, he wrote, he loved."[9] Love grows out of expertise. Expertise in what? Well, I'm going to use a word that . . . oh, too bad: in magic! That's right, it's magic, or something like magic. Now you don't come across magical people very often, but still, there are a few. It's in Shakespeare, you know, magic, so there you go. Mustn't say it too loud, but it's true for a fact, love consists in making magic. White magic, of course: when it's black, it's dreadful. Magic exists: there are fairies and there are witches. I prefer fairies.

BB: Julia, in *Tales of Love*, you suggest that deep down all human stories are love stories. After all, if there's one subject we never tire of, it's that one! With regard to the topic that has brought us here tonight—"Love of the other"—I might perhaps formulate the matter another way: the incredibly strong and beautiful experience you just described lifts one out of oneself, out of one's territory, to approach the foreignness of the other, forge ties to the other, to their difference. It makes us bring a different gaze to bear on those around us and on our relationships with others. In our fragmented societies, too many walls are put up, boundaries, exclusions. You mentioned them in the context of young Julia's arrival in France, but it seems to me that this has hardly changed. In fact, it's become worse.

JK: Is love implicated in the social realm, or not? Can there be any possible deployment or extension of amorous logics across the public sphere? I'll start my attempt at an answer by emphasizing, firstly, as ever, the *destructiveness* which love is helpless to staunch or eradicate; the best love can do is adjust it, contain it, or, best of all, sublimate it. Hatred never disappears in love nor in ourselves as speaking creatures: all living beings have aggressive *urges*, and humans of both sexes are inhabited by *affects* consisting of urges accompanied by psychic representation, and, of these, *hate* is older than love. This is something discovered by psychoanalysis; could that be one reason for the distrust leveled toward it by religious and even humanist moralisms? What's more, the hate object, unlike the love object, never disappoints. Sentimental idealism imposes the myth of "pure love" (I'm thinking of quietists like Mme Guyon). However, as soon as the love bond acknowledges the partner's foreignness and "plays the game" as a doubles match (taking the psychic bisexuality of both sides on board), then aggression and hatred rise to the surface again.

BB: But doesn't "love of the other" save us from experiencing ourselves as foreign or alien?

JK: Foreign, alien? Right from the start, I realized that my conduct in love, too, had to be of a kind suited to times of war. I found out much later that "my" saint, Teresa of Avila, thought the same way. "I don't agree with you": on the subject of China, perhaps, embraced by Philippe with all his vast cultural memory, so that he's apt to transfigure the constraints of global finance and Confucian bureaucracy; or maybe on the subject of humanism, skewered by Philippe as flabby thinking, while he mocks my wish to refound it through the transvaluation of religious legacies—well, you can imagine the furious rages that erupt between us in the course of such apparently abstract disputes . . . Our tempers are just as much fired by disagreements over our social circles or the elections or celebrities, etc. And yet our clear-cut positions eventually align into harmony without necessarily getting planed down.

Because long-term love, the kind I'm talking about, is tantamount to a continuation of the war between the sexes, conducted through other means: reciprocity, connection, affection, desire . . . And forgiveness also has its place, not effacing the hostilities-aggressions-hatreds but "interpreting" them—if I may use a technical term. Interpretation in day-to-day life takes the form of clarification: recall of past history, understanding of limits, tact, also laughter, and . . . silence!

I am speaking of a love that comprehends the *crossing* of the impossible: neither denial nor acceptance. The word *silence* seems fitting for this dimension of the alchemy of love. I'd like to read, apropos of that, a passage from a novel I recently completed, *The Enchanted Clock*.[10]

Have you heard the absolute silence that thrums over the Earth, just before the fall of night? It can only be picked up by an ear straining for the deep radiance of beings, oblivious to interference. What is called a couple, in the inaccessible sense of the word, is formed when two people hear that radiance in themselves, in each other, and in the world around. Nobody else can enter in. So we became a kind of couple, he and I.

There. Thank you. And if one can't bear that silence or can't hear it—because it's not a matter of endurance but of hearing, accompanying, seeing it, even . . .

BB: Not being afraid of it . . .

JK: Not being afraid of it, that's right. If that silent chord is missing, nothing's happening. Yes, the attunement of silences: the secret of composition.

PS: That's what music is!

JK: From that point on, in the psychic space thus constructed in tandem, movements and actions may unfold that, notwithstanding their private nature, also have a social implication—coming back to the "fragmented societies" you mentioned before, Bernadette. Responsibility, solidarity, care, friendship, these become more lucid and committed, as much between ourselves as with our close relatives, colleagues, and friends, or in civic involvement. And let's not forget parenthood, which is absolutely crucial: our closeness to our son David, to his early learning, his schooling, his love affairs, his coming to maturity . . . The underlying love experience is refracted through such multiple facets of our "living together," as people say now. And do you know what it all leads to, this depth and diffusion of love? To work, to works, and to actions . . . Work, works, actions . . . That's all. Clearly.

In the end, you've brought me from the deeps to the surface, and I realize that I'm talking about a love that's not *paraded*. One that stands apart from *chimera love*, I'd say, in the intelligence or plenitude of love, in a place that is not always accessible to what's commonly called "love." What should it be called, then? An insight from "my" Teresa comes to mind: "We cannot be liberated from demons without being liberated from God, that is, from love." Well, then, perhaps the crimes and technologies of modern times invite us to chase after demons, to transvalue the divine, and, without liberating us *from* love, to *liberate love*, infinitely. To become the point where this infinite liberation acquires body and meaning.

AUDIENCE MEMBER: How do you account for the many people in this world who only live to hate? Hitler, Le Pen, what's the matter with these people who care for nothing but intolerance and hatred?

PS: Ah, yes, hatred . . . The more you hear of *love* bandied about in vacuous, rom-com, show-biz, magazine-flogging, commodified terms, be warned, the more hatred lurks beneath. The falser the love—and it's very seldom genuine, by the way—the greater the hate, which is older than love, as Freud points out. Lacan came up with a very fine formula which is his concept of *hainamoration*, "hatelove": a form of love, but love unto death, crazy love. Not *amour fou* in the surrealist sense; Breton's book of that title is a magnificent work; Breton stands for freedom, love, and poetry. What I should have said earlier is that, for me, love *is* freedom; it's the opposite of slavery. Hate, Madam questioner, well, yes, it keeps popping up, over and over: look, there it is again. But I don't see why everyone gives it so much publicity. For example, I find it very strange how people keep going on about the Front National, however critically. If I had the power, something God forbid, I'd put a stop to it: new subject! Haven't you got anything else to talk about? There are periods, I feel, when the whole world rushes with righteous and hypocritical indignation to denounce hatred, racism, anti-semitism, and all that. It rings curiously false; to my ears, it's like everybody wants the same thing. Of course, they'll say, "Oh, not at all!" but, when I hear "Not at all!" chorused over and over on every TV channel, I get a weird feeling, and that's what I'm feeling now as I try to give you an answer.

BB: The questioner was wondering how we should confront the various fanaticisms that inspire people to commit crimes against humanity. Can psychoanalysis offer a resource against hate?

JK: What I've attempted to express tonight is based on my personal experience, but it won't have escaped your notice that psycho-analysis has been subjacent throughout, with Freud often being cited, even though I didn't always make my allusions explicit. Allow me to insist on the point. By putting symptoms and trau-mas on the couch, Freud turned amorous folly, amorous failure, want of love, and hate itself into objects of observation or, better said, of interpretation; in other words, of *forgiveness*. The word should be written with a hyphen: to *for-give*[11]—to give meaning to the ill-being that is rooted in your particular love disaster. It can be achieved if we transfer love on the couch, you and I, during our encounter; if we try to elucidate, revive, and rebirth it, make it new again. It doesn't always work, but it can work: for-giveness opens up time to infinity.

Because, unlike religious forgiveness, interpretation dur-ing transference does not *erase* or *suspend* the ill-being, the fault, the guilt, or even the crime, it merely elucidates and strives to unpick them. Lacan put us on guard: psychoanalysis must not become an "understanding moralism." Instead, an accompanying—a companionship in love, if I may put it like that. On condition of taking that concept to the edge of the unconscious and of biology, where war, hatred, laughter, and silence play out. A unique companionship, tailored to each individual, to help one become once more capable of forging the ties of love, according to a greater or lesser aptitude for this infinite reconstruction.

If you've followed me thus far, it will be clear that psychoanalysis, as I understand it, with and after Freud, has something to say to religions, nationalisms, and fundamentalisms. All of them, in effect, expound "lovers' discourses"—about God, the identity of a people, the absolute—that are clenched into hatred of the other, of identity, of the nation, of the absolute . . .

BB: You were recently at the University of Haifa, where you delivered a lecture on "the new forms of revolt."

JK: These forms include gangster fundamentalism or jihadism. The spreaders of this "radical ailment" are mostly very young men, fragile, uncertain youths; but there are also splintered adults, prey to the same yearning for ideals and hunger for absolute satisfaction, "madmen of God" and/or of love. In this way I seek to underline, along with Kant and Arendt, the propensity of some human beings to declare other human beings superfluous and set about exterminating them. Wars without front lines, viral wars are breaking out in our cities, subways, Jewish schools, editorial offices; hostages are beheaded and the inevitable videos posted, to instill abject terror in miscreants around the world.

These fanatics, patching up their crumbling psyches with odds and ends of religion taken to extremes, these gangster fundamentalists who have lost all sense of right and wrong, of self and other, of inside and outside, embody a real anthropological disintegration and thus a radical phase of the nihilism that threatens all globalized cultures. Family breakdown; displacement or exile; educational failure; unfulfilling jobs, social discrimination, and sexual frustration, all these whip them into near-hypnotic states, bereft of both the self and the other: *desubjectified* and *deobjectified* at once. It's no solution condemning and bombing them while exhibiting them onscreen before, during, or after a decapitation as they revel in the victim's humiliation and death. It is possible to preempt this dehumanization: to step in as soon as a child seems disturbed at school, in the community. It's not true to say that they were "average, normal kids" and "nobody noticed anything wrong."

PS: The important thing here is the refusal of difference.

JK: The fanatic's "difference," which is the compensation of pain in maniacal mode, exalting a wishful neoreality, climaxes with the fantasy of an absolute paradise—possession of every female, access to every amenity, lavish wealth, compliant and restorative community, etc.—in short, total Love on tap. In this unbounded neoreality, killing acs like a drug, on top of the substance abuse encouraged by the arms and drugs mafias. In my view, of all the "sciences of the mind," psychoanalysis is the best equipped to spot and diagnose such dangers before their morbid effects take hold. And it's through the analyst's involvement in transference—that is, through the therapist's psychic affective proximity and her clinical knowledge of this *radical illness*, that she or he can become the linchpin of the process of screening and accompanying these morbid agents engaged in their viral war on civilization. Because, I repeat, analytic interpretation is consubstantial with the transference-countertransference love upon which it relies and from which it springs.

Who pays for this individual, customized attention, I hear you ask? The state, of course, if it is truly committed to a secularism that requires citizens to be *formed*, not just *formatted* into webnauts brought up on the blissful slogans of Internet advertising—the mirror image of jihadist propaganda, minus its promise of shortcuts to Heaven.

AUDIENCE MEMBER: What do you think of Lacan's statement, that "love is giving something one doesn't have to a person who doesn't want it"?

PS: Too pessimistic!

JK: Lacan was a good friend of mine, and I read him a great deal and attended the Seminar, but I grew away from him in his later years: I discussed this in an interview with *L'Express*, "The Lacan Event" (2011).¹²

I often felt he was misunderstood by those he cared for, unlucky in love. The sentence you quoted, like the one where he says "There is no such thing as sexual rapport," was targeting the fantasies of complete fulfillment harbored by lovers who deny *lack* and the set of *negative emotions* at work in the sexual act and the bond of love. Furthermore, in his theory, the role of instinctual urges and the investment of *transference* by the analyst's *countertransference* are not given their due place. As for jouissance, which according to him can't be uttered— any more than truth—it seems to me that both the history of literature and the ethics of psychoanalysis have set themselves the challenge of uttering and writing it: without end in sight, certainly, but without restrictions either. His assertion that in love "one gives something one doesn't have to someone who doesn't want it" is only valid for the dance, or trance, of seduction. There are lasting love relationships, of the kind we've discussed tonight, that go beyond this vaudeville. These other forms of loving, while always being errant, search and innovate by means of a sensitive, reciprocal intelligence, to which the love you were referring to has no real access.

Am I so optimistic, then? I often define myself as an energetic pessimist.

NOTES

PREFACE: ADVENTURE

1. This essay, which precedes the 1946 edition of *L'Âge d'homme*, is known in English as *The Autobiographer as Torero*—Trans.

PREFACE: HARMONIZING OUR FOREIGNNESSES

1. Sollers commentates this phrase by Stéphane Mallarmé in the preface to his novel, *Une curieuse solitude* (Paris: Seuil, 1958; Points Seuil, 2001); *A Strange Solitude*, trans. Richard Howard (London: Eyre and Spottiswood, 1961).

I. COMPLICITY, LAUGHTER, HURT

Interview with François Armanet and Sylvie Véran for *Le Nouvel Observateur*, August 1996.

1. In English in the original—Trans.

2. INNER EXPERIENCE AGAINST THE CURRENT

This conversation took place in the Réfectoire des Cordeliers in Paris on April 27, 2011, as part of the "Entretiens des Grands Moulins" series directed by Bernadette Bricout, vice president for culture at the University of Paris-7 Diderot. The moderator was Colette Fellous, a writer and a producer at Radio France Culture.

1. *Le Vieil Homme et les loups* (Paris: Fayard, 1991); *The Old Man and the Wolves*, trans. Barbara Bray (New York: Columbia University Press, 1994).

2. *Drame* (Seuil, 1965; Gallimard, L'Imaginaire, 1990). *Event*, trans. B. Benderson and U. Molinaro (New York: Red Dust, 1986).

3. *Histoires d'amour* (Paris: Denoël, 1983 and Folio Essais no. 24, 1985); *Tales of Love*, trans. Leon S. Roudiez (New York: Columbia University Press, 1987).

4. Martin Heidegger, "Hegels Begriff der Erfahrung," in *Holzwege* (Frankfurt: Vittorio Klostermann, 1950), included in *Martin Heidegger: Off the Beaten Track*, ed. and trans. Julian Young and Kenneth Haynes (Cambridge: Cambridge University Press, 2002).

5. The Lacanian concept of *hainamoration*. See p. 90.

6. *Des Chinoises* (Paris: des femmes, 1974, rev. ed. Paris: Pauvert, 2005). *About Chinese Women*, trans. Anita Barrows (London: Marion Boyars, 1977, rpt. 2000).

7. International Psychoanalytical Association.

8. "Hyperbole! Can you not rise / In triumph from my memory, / A modern magic spell devise / As from an ironbound grammary." Stéphane Mallarmé, *Collected Poems*, trans. Henry Weinfield (Berkeley: University of California Press, 1994).

9. *Le temps sensible. Proust et l'expérience littéraire* (Paris: Gallimard, 1994 and Folio Essais, 2000); *Proust and the Sense of Time*, trans. Stephen Bann (New York: Columbia University Press, 1993).

10. Sollers, *Event*.

11. *Les Nouvelles Maladies de l'âme* (Fayard, 1993 and Livre de Poche, 1997); *New Maladies of the Soul*, trans. Ross Guberman (New York: Columbia University Press, 1997).

12. *Oublire* is a portmanteau of *oublier* (to forget) and *lire* (to read). *Vous m'avez oublu* would be something like "You've *forread* or *oblivioread* me"—TRANS.

13. In French, Sollers says "le '*temporer*' de Heidegger." This is Sollers's translation, in his 1978 essay "Paradis," of Heidegger's neologistic verbalization of the noun in *Unterwegs zur Sprache* (1959): "Die Zeit zeitigt"—TRANS.

14. "Bulgarie, ma souffrance," *L'Infini* 51 (Fall 1995): 42–52; "Bulgaria, My Suffering," in Kristeva, *Crisis of the European Subject*, trans. Susan Fairfield (New York: Other Press, 2000), pp. 163–83. See also "The Future of Revolt," in *Intimate Revolt*, trans. Jeanine Herman (New York: Columbia University Press, 2003).

15. Julia Kristeva and Jean Vanier, *Leur regard perce nos ombres* (Paris: Fayard, 2011).

16. In the original French, the neological infinitive *temper*, from the noun *temps*, "time"—TRANS.

17. Philippe Sollers, *Les Voyageurs du Temps* (Paris: Gallimard, 2009, Folio, 2012).

18. In English in the original—TRANS.

3. CHILDHOOD AND YOUTH OF A FRENCH WRITER

Contribution to the encounter around Philippe Sollers convened on June 29, 2010, by Father Antoine Guggenheim, director of the research center of the Collège des Bernardins in Paris, the Cistercian monastery restored and reopened in 2008 on the initiative of the late Cardinal Lustiger. A first version of the text appeared in *L'Infini* 112 (Fall 2010).

1. *Le Parc* (Paris: Seuil, 1961); *The Park*, trans. A. M. Sheridan Smith (New York: Red Dust, 1977); *Lois* (Paris: Seuil, 1972); *H* (Paris: Seuil, 1973); *H*, trans. V. Stankovianska and D. Vichnar (London: Equus, 2015); *Paradis* (Paris: Seuil, 1981); *La Guerre du goût* (Paris: Gallimard, 1994); *Une vie divine* (Paris: Gallimard, 2006); *La Fête à Venise* (Paris: Gallimard, 1991); *Watteau in Venice*, trans. Alberto Manguel (New York: Scribner's, 1994); *Un vrai roman: Mémoires* (Paris: Plon, 2007); *Discours Parfait* (Paris: Gallimard, 2010).

2. An allusion to the title of Michel Braudeau's review of *La Fête à Venise* in *Le Monde*, February 1, 1991.

3. In English in the original—TRANS.

4. *Folies françaises* (Paris: Gallimard, 1988).

5. Friedrich Hölderlin, "Andenken" (1803), in *Vaterländische Gesänge* (1846). Philippe Sollers alludes to that poem, "Remembrance," in his discussion of Heidegger's lectures on Hölderlin, *Approche de Hölderlin*

(Paris: Gallimard, 1951); Martin Heidegger, *Elucidations of Hölderlin's Poetry*, trans. Keith Hoeller (Amherst: Humanity, 2000).

6. Homer, *The Odyssey*, book 1, trans. Robert Fagles (London: Penguin, 1997), p. 77.

7. Cf. Julia Kristeva, "L'adolescence, un syndrome d'idéalité," in *La Haine et le Pardon*, (Paris: Fayard, 2005), pp. 447–60, translated by Jeanine Herman as *Hatred and Forgiveness* (New York: Columbia University Press, 2010).

8. Charles Baudelaire, "An Opium Eater," in *Artificial Paradises*, trans. Stacy Diamond (New York: Citadel, 1996), p. 137.

9. Alphonse de Lamartine (1790–1869), *Méditations II*, 15, "Les Préludes."

10. Charles Baudelaire, *The Painter of Modern Life* (1863): "But genius is nothing more nor less than childhood recovered at will—a childhood now equipped for self-expression with manhood's capacities and a power of analysis which enables it to order the mass of raw material which it has involuntarily accumulated." Trans. Jonathan Mayne (London: Phaidon, 1995), p. 8.

11. Georges Bernanos (1888–1948), *Dialogue des Carmélites* (1949), in *Œuvres romanesques* (Paris: Gallimard, Bibliothèque de la Pléiade, 1961), p. 1586.

12. A frequent expression in Daoism. Cf. Lao Tzu, *Tao Te Ching*, I, 10.

13. Philippe Sollers, *Femmes* (Paris: Gallimard, 1983); *Women*, trans. Barbara Bray (New York: Columbia University Press, 1009).

14. Friedrich Nietzsche (1844–1900), "Thus Spoke Zarathustra," in *Ecce Homo*, trans. Duncan Large (Oxford: Oxford World's Classics, 2007), p. 68.

15. Sollers, *Une vie divine*.

16. Ibid.

4. LOVE OF THE OTHER

The chair is Bernadette Bricout, vice president of the University of Paris-7 Diderot (with responsibility for cultural life and the university in the city). She started among other projects the series of talks, "Entretiens des Grands Moulins," the framework for the "Inner Experience Against the Current" event, held on April 27, 2011. The present occasion was an evening held on June 19, 2014, at the Cercle Bernard-Lazare in Paris, on the topic "Love of the Other."

1. *Tales of Love*, trans. Leon S. Roudiez (New York: Columbia University Press, 1987).

2. In English in the original—TRANS.

3. *Les Samouraïs* (Paris: Fayard, 1990); *The Samurai*, trans. Barbara Bray (New York: Columbia University Press, 1992).

4. *Étrangers à nous-mêmes* (Paris: Fayard, 1988); *Strangers to Ourselves*, trans. Leon S. Roudiez (New York: Columbia University Press, 1991).

5. Roland Barthes, "L'Étrangère," first published in *La Quinzaine littéraire*, no. 94 May 1–15, 1970. See also Barthes, *Œuvres complètes*, ed. and intro. Éric Marty, 3 vols. (Paris: Seuil, 1993–195), 2:860–62.

6. *The Old Man and the Wolves*, trans. Barbara Bray (New York: Columbia University Press, 1994)

7. *Trésor d'amour* (Paris: Gallimard, 2011).

8. *A Strange Solitude*, trans. Richard Howard (London: Eyre and Spottiswood, 1961), p. 14.

9. *Visse, scrisse, amò*.

10. *L'Horloge enchantée* (Paris: Fayard, 2015).

11. In French, *le par-don*, literally "by-gift"—TRANS.

12. Cf. *Pulsions du temps* (Paris: Fayard, 2013), pp. 259–66.